Praise for *Holy Guacamole*

"I planned to skim this bo  COULD
NOT PUT IT DOWN! enged and
excited about tapping int My friend
Carrie 'gets it,' and through ɔ truth, we
get a big dose of refreshment and courage to live more alive every day."
–Lynette Lewis, TEDx speaker, pastor's wife,
author of *Climbing the Ladder in Stilettos*

"It has been a privilege to work with Carrie (and Morgan, her husband) in church planting, campus ministry, and world mission for over two decades. During this time, I have watched Carrie lead in the same way she writes—with faith, hope, love, and a unique sense of humor. I trust that this book will deepen your walk with Christ and challenge you to see your intrinsic value to God and His church. I am thankful for her voice."
–Steve Murrell, President of Every Nation Churches & Ministries

"Carrie Stephens uses humor and grace to help readers see themselves how Jesus sees them—messy, human, and oh-so-valuable. If you're looking for a whole lot of encouragement—and a whole lot of laughter—grab this book, a notebook and a pen, and soak up the grace."
–Erin MacPherson, author of 11 books including
Put the Disciple into Discipline

"This book is vulnerable, authentic, powerful, and hilarious. Each chapter is full of relatable Bible exposition, personal experience, and references for just about everything. Carrie puts them together in just the right portions, keeping her reader hooked as she captures life in all its beautiful messiness. Read it and draw encouragement from the fact that you too are *Holy Guacamole*."
–Joseph Bonafacio, Lead Pastor of Victory Katipunan,
Director of Every Nation Campus - Philippines

"*Holy Guacamole* puts a fun spin on the real complexities of marriage, motherhood, and ministry. Carrie takes readers on a hilariously transparent journey, making space for the frustrations and joys that are sometimes hard to articulate. Read this book if, like us, you're navigating all of the weird places of life's transitions and trying to discover where you fit in again."
–Terry and Ashley Williams, Owners of The League
Gym & Serial Entrepreneurs

"Through absurd yet relatable metaphors, this book is filled with humor as fresh as a bowl of tableside guacamole. You won't even realize how many invaluable life lessons you've learned after you've spent the majority of this book rolling on the floor laughing. All jokes aside, if you admire an author with unparalleled humility and obedience to God, you need to read this."

–Adrian Crawford, Founder of Engage Church
and The New Rules Collective

"Carrie gives a fully transparent, abundantly humorous, and extremely relatable account of her journey in life and leadership. I found myself going back and forth between laughing along and nodding my head with many of her experiences and revelations. If you've ever felt like an afterthought in God's greater plan, or like your life is too mundane to matter, this book will bless you with a better truth."

–Seth Trimmer, Lead Pastor Grace City Church

"So much of this book resonated with deep longings of my heart that have been modestly tucked and back-burnered by the often misrepresented expectations that surround womanhood, leadership, and motherhood—especially in the Church. Carrie's words cut right into the heart of what women in the church have all been thinking yet were too afraid, or perhaps ashamed, to voice aloud. Her words are spot on—bold, unapologetic, yet also saturated with humility and grace.

As a 3rd-row pew observer of pastor's wives for years, I always peered over at the back of First Lady heads, assuming they were surely walking Proverbs 31 women, carrying the entire 'How to be a Woman of God' playbook in their back pocket. Carrie debunks this in a way I never knew I needed. I'm grateful to see her humanness connect with my humanness. In *Holy Guacamole*, a part of me exhales, knowing that as women of God, we are all just being carried daily by the grace of Jesus. We are the *Holy Guacamole*—not the side rice and beans—we are worthy, invited, desired, and enough in Christ!"

–Tania Woods, Founder & Editor of Inkfully.com
and the Inkfully Podcast

A GLORIOUS DISCOVERY
OF YOUR UNDENIABLE WORTH

CARRIE STEPHENS

SHILOH RUN  PRESS
An Imprint of Barbour Publishing, Inc.

Print ISBN 978-1-64352-299-9

eBook Editions:
Adobe Digital Edition (.epub) 978-1-64352-571-6
Kindle and MobiPocket Edition (.prc) 978-1-64352-572-3

Cover Art: Kristin Duran
Cover Design: Greg Jackson, Thinkpen Design

Published in association with Jessica Kirkland and the literary agency of Kirkland Media Management, LLC. P.O. Box 1539, Liberty, Texas 77575.

Published by Shiloh Run Press, an imprint of Barbour Publishing, Inc., 1810 Barbour Drive, Uhrichsville, Ohio 44683, www.shilohrunpress.com

Our mission is to inspire the world with the life-changing message of the Bible.

Member of the
Evangelical Christian
Publishers Association

Printed in the United States of America.

DEDICATION

For everyone seeking a way through.

CONTENTS

HELLO, MY NAME IS CARRIE AND I AM A SECRET DONUT HOARDER

When one of my sons was a toddler, his temperament was something along the lines of "unexpectedly unhinged." One afternoon he awoke from a nap desperate for something. He had no words back then, just strange babble that made no sense to my husband or me.

We frantically tried to figure out what he needed. We got him his favorite blanket. He continued screaming. We held him and spoke soothingly to him. He became more hysterical. We made him a sippy cup of chocolate milk. Full-out shrieking ensued, and he swatted the cup out of my hand like it was poison.

The situation had clearly moved from trying to dire.

My husband, Morgan, looked at me and said, "Good Lord, what's wrong with him?"

"I don't know," I said. "But as bad as it is to deal with him out here, it's got to be way worse inside his head."

Morgan nodded and said, "Ah, yes. *It comes from within.*"

Indeed, it does.

As all of my children have now progressed through the stages of early childhood and are currently climbing the steep path through puberty, trying their wings in the teenage season of preadulting, I often think of that day. Teens are as capable of instability as nonverbal preschoolers. But it's not only my kids who are unhinged. As I counsel people in our church who face impossible situations, I see my two-year-old son's desperation in their eyes. When I roll down my window to greet the woman flying a sign on the corner, I hear my child's longing in her voice.

We are all that inconsolable child sometimes. We can't quite explain what's happening in our inner world. We are desperate for something, but we don't always know what we really need. And we frequently lash out at the people trying to help us.

In the pages of this book, you will find some of my thoughts on the challenges of life, as well as the kind of hope God offers us in the midst of it all. I hope that when you find yourself in these stories, you will also feel the presence of God and His endless love for you. Christ is always with you, you know. He is the breath in your lungs and the light dawning just when you need it most.

I also hope you will laugh as you read, because while God's love for you is serious business, none of us should take ourselves too seriously. And for goodness' sake, drink some chocolate milk and eat a few donuts while you read (personally, I always order a dozen hot donut holes and pretend they're for everyone to share, but then I eat them all because the YOLO donut life feels like winning).

We'll get to the winning part later. For now, I really need to tell you about my stupid refrigerator.

CHAPTER 1

From the Well to the Ice Maker

Embracing the Truth about Our Lives

ONE TIME MY REFRIGERATOR BROKE. I LITERALLY
DIDN'T KNOW WHAT TO DO! I JUST MOVED.
TOM HAVERFORD, *PARKS AND RECREATION*

I'm just a girl, standing in front of her refrigerator, asking Jesus to fix it.

My refrigerator broke into pieces when my parents came over for dinner one night. My dad opened the refrigerator door, and a shard about the size of my hand broke off one of the shelves and fell to the floor. We just stood there and stared at it, pondering the possibility that this shattered shelf was a prophetic signal.

Thus says the Lord, "You cannot handle the weight of your life. . . ."

Indeed, nothing says, "Mom, Dad, your worst fears are true. I'll never be a fully functioning adult. You will never stop worrying about me. Not ever," quite like having a piece of a major appliance in your home fly out and land at your dad's feet.

"Uh, I think you've got a problem here," my dad said and winked at me mischievously.

This lovely father-daughter moment reminded me a lot of the day the previous summer when he and I used an old dish towel, six inches of duct tape, and a piece of plastic wrap to plug up the dispenser for my fridge's ice maker so it would stop leaking water all over my kitchen floor. I rewarded him afterward with a plate of cookies.

It's a good thing that refrigerators aren't such a *crucial* part of our everyday lives here in the Western world, you know? It is a *bless*ing that Old Silver (as I've so lovingly named it) keeps breaking so my dad and I can have these precious moments together watching YouTube repair videos. It means I can say things like, "Hold on a second, kids, this cute photo of Grandpa and me next to Old Silver is destined for the 'gram" (#foreverlove #daddysgirl #bonding #thedaysarelongbuthe yearsareshort).

This new father-daughter teamwork thing is possible because after living eleven hundred miles away from us for most of my adult life, my mom and dad moved into our neighborhood in the spring of 2017. People often either cringe or sigh when I mention this.

I suppose it could be challenging to have your parents move in around the corner right when you hit your midlife crisis. I mean, I've watched every episode of *Everybody Loves Raymond*, and I can see how it might be particularly sticky for my husband, Morgan, to have his in-laws so close. Thankfully, my family is still in awe that someone as amazing as Morgan would voluntarily attach himself to me with only death as a possible way out of the arrangement. When Morgan called my dad in November of 2000 and told him he planned to propose, my dad had one response: "She's all yours." Morgan has reached sainthood in my family for loving me and enduring my nonsense.

If asked, my parents could probably tell you that I wasn't

always as easygoing as I am now that I'm in full-blown midlife crisis mode, with an eroding refrigerator and a helter-skelter hormonal balance. Growing up, I was a moody and complicated girl who was frequently disappointed when her fantastical expectations of life never quite materialized. I was a delight to be around when puberty rode in like a Mack truck without brakes. I had an eye for designer everything—such a joy to parents on a "beer budget," as my dad put it. However, I gave up alcohol altogether a couple of decades ago, and I like to think I've become stable and easy to please in my forties.

(I like to think it, but that doesn't make it true.)

What *is* true is that when my parents moved into our neighborhood, our lives got a massive upgrade. My mom takes care of our family like Jesus Himself has given her the keys to our happiness. She fills in when we need dinner or another kid chauffeur, and she cheers at my kids' baseball games like they're one game away from the World Series. My dad fixed my son's bike seventy-eight times in nine months. He also helped me replace the broken handle on my car door and build shelves above my washer and dryer. Dad installed cabinet hardware in my kitchen and bathrooms. He's oiled squeaky hinges and fiddled with garage doors to literally make our lives run more smoothly. Of course, I already mentioned the MacGyver ice maker fix. I estimate that my dad has saved us a few thousand dollars in repair and handyman bills since my parents relocated to Texas.

However, even the best parents in the world can't fix everything or pick up enough slack to make the hardest parts of life easy.

So, on that accursed night when Old Silver broke apart, once the fajita platters were empty and my parents headed home, I held the shard of the shelf in my hand and stared into the depths of the broken beast. Not the bright, young stainless fridge she once was, her quality of life had been declining the past couple of years. A massive crack split the shelf holding the milk down its middle. Reaching into the vegetable bins had become akin to a game of *Fear Factor* since the interior lights went out: you might get slimed. . .or worse. Without the ability to regulate temperature, Old Silver had been accidentally freezing the lettuce regularly. I'd called repairmen twice to keep her up and running, but now I regretted spending the money. Old Silver had forgotten her God-ordained calling to keep our perishables cool, not to mention her completely incontinent ice maker. Clearly she longed for greener pastures, or maybe just to be retired to the garage to serve our family as a water and soda fridge.

All of this is how I came to be a girl (okay, middle-aged woman) standing in front of her refrigerator, asking Jesus to fix the shelf and the ice maker and every other broken thing I've been ignoring. If I'm going to ask for a miracle, I might as well go for glory.

ON THE EIGHTH DAY, GOD DID NOT MAKE DUCT TAPE

All this broken appliance talk has me thinking about the day Jesus sat down at a well in Samaria, and a Samaritan woman showed up. The refrigerator could pretty much be considered the modern well, after all. Everyone needed the local well in the ancient Middle East, just as all the people in our house need Old Silver for life-sustaining supplies like Topo Chico[1] and Gatorade. The story begins with this:

---

[1] If you aren't familiar with Topo Chico, which is the most amazing sparkling water in the world, I pity you. If you hate sparkling water, I have already shed tears that you could lose so much joy so effortlessly in life.

A woman from Samaria came to draw water. Jesus said to her, "Give me a drink.". . . The Samaritan woman said to him, "How is it that you, a Jew, ask for a drink from me, a woman of Samaria?" (For Jews have no dealings with Samaritans.) Jesus answered her, "If you knew the gift of God, and who it is that is saying to you, 'Give me a drink,' you would have asked him, and he would have given you living water. . . . Everyone who drinks of this water will be thirsty again, but whoever drinks of the water that I will give him will never be thirsty again. The water that I will give him will become in him a spring of water welling up to eternal life." The woman said to him, "Sir, give me this water, so that I will not be thirsty or have to come here to draw water."
(John 4:7, 9–10, 13–15 ESV)

Then Jesus told her everything about her life, how she had never found a man who would be faithful to her. He revealed His true identity as the Messiah, which stands out as a rare moment of definitive truth in the stories about Jesus. All this happened because she showed up at a well, the place a woman in ancient times had to go to get what she needed to survive another day.

Similarly, peering into my broken refrigerator has exposed all the broken pieces in my soul and in the world. I'm suddenly aware of all sorts of things I need God to fix. There are other broken appliances in our house; our dryer is on the fritz, and the dishwasher keeps filling up with mold. But my friends also need healing, our country feels more broken every time I turn on the news, and I have a whole host of insecurities I'm trying to sort out.

The question demanding answers is this: What do we do with our brokenness when we're forced to hold it in our hands? Where should I put the shard of the shelf that fell out? What kind of glue works in freezing temperatures? I'd like to read the back of our tube of magic glue for instructions, but my reading vision stinks now that I've breached forty. My old lady eyes can't tell the difference between the tube of glue and the eye cream I keep in the bathroom. I'm terrified of mixing the two up someday. How awful would it be if I got eye cream and glue mixed up?[2]

The trail from the ice to the glue to the eye cream leads me to the truth about what's happening: Jesus is here, by my broken refrigerator, to tell me everything about myself—just like He did with the woman at the well. I am an awful lot like her and like my refrigerator: broken and in need of help. I have been gluing myself back together for years with creams and serums and some weird thing that pokes me with a dozen little needles so that the lotion can "penetrate and erase" the fine lines around my eyes. I still look relatively shiny on the outside, but when you open me up and take a good look, there are parts of me that are slightly cracked and not as functional as they ought to be.

When I think of my friends and neighbors, I realize there are all sorts of things holding us together. We are each a conglomeration of soul glues, dysfunctional duct tapes, emotional bungees, and spiritual straps. We go through our days seeing ads on television that promise we would be happy and everyone would love us *if only* we could afford to buy this one thing. We listen to the pithy advice of our culture, which promises

---

[2] Although this may be a way to go viral on YouTube and promote this book. Alexa, file the idea under "desperate book launch ideas."

us that *if only* we could achieve a little more success, then the inadequacy that is slowly crushing us would dissipate. We tape up all our fears and insecurities and begin to believe the hardness of life would flee *if only* we looked a little more like supermodels. *If only* we could each find a spouse exactly like the dreamy (albeit fictional) character on-screen. *If only* we had friends who understood and loved our true selves. Our brokenness is playing hide-and-seek behind all the if onlys, and until we let it safely come out of hiding, we will spend our days chasing another easy fix to a truly cosmic problem.

While the world continually suggests we muster up one more thing to become the people we really want to be, more hustle can't give new life to my old refrigerator or bring back the glorious skin of my twenties. Despite what social media's curated posts and "inspirational" memes may declare, more hustle and better hype can't bring peace in the midst of the storms of life, cure the sicknesses of our societies, or teach us to love one another as Christ has loved us. The quest to keep our brokenness securely taped behind a shiny exterior of performance and perfection has tricked us into thinking we can create a life for ourselves apart from our Creator God.

Besides, the hustle is exhausting, isn't it?

In front of my refrigerator with Jesus, I see He's offering all of us something far better than hustle. Come and see this Christ, who can tell us everything about our lives. He has living water that can quench our thirst for an end to the hustle for greatness and significance.

We don't need tape or glue to hold it all together. We don't have to manufacture or birth another ounce of self-love to make it through the day. Contrary to every self-help book out there, I want to tell you the most profound truth: *You can never save yourself through self-improvement.* Self-improvement may help you grow and develop in your relationships and as a leader, but it can't make your eternity more secure. Your joy and fulfillment are not contingent upon you "doing you" in the most real and glorious way you can find. God has far more beautiful plans for us than improving our self-image so we will feel more confident and self-assured.

Jesus doesn't offer us access to better water just so we won't be so thirsty for love and approval all the time. He's offering us a kind of love and belonging that will release springs of living water inside us so we will never thirst again.

CONCEALER, CONTOURS, AND GOOD FOUNDATION

As with the Samaritan woman, our encounters with Jesus force questions upon us. *Can we relinquish control of our lives to God and trust Him? How do we embrace our imperfections without losing all sense of our value? Will everything really be okay if we let go of our identity safety nets and backup plans?*

I've been asking myself these things ever since I turned thirty-five. That was when it became apparent that for all my life I had blissfully assumed old people spawned somehow from the dust of the earth—and I'd been wrong. I also realized that every day is for keeps. If I don't cling to Jesus in this time and in this place, I will miss out on all He has for me here and possibly end up somewhere I don't want to be in twenty years.

Before my midthirties I never looked at a wrinkled face and thought, *Jesus and I will be there together one day.* I was pretentious enough to believe I had some control over time, I guess. I would stay young forever. I had never faced any aging problems before, so why would I have them in the future? The gray-haired people I saw everywhere were lovely, but they were nothing like me. I was going from glory to glory! I couldn't fathom a day when I would be staring at the roots of my hair and realizing they were no longer dark blond.[3] Future regrets weren't even in the realm of possibility.

Nevertheless, as that great prophet Smash Mouth taught us: the years start coming at you whether you like it or not—and they don't stop coming just because you want to stay forever young. My ninety-year-old grandmother tells me this is truer than I can fathom.

Every middle-aged person got here the same way I did. Every gray-haired lady got here just as my grandmother did. One day at a time. We were all young and smooth and toned(ish) at some point. Once upon a time, we didn't need fish oil to help with achy hips or collagen powder smoothies to aid our digestion. We didn't need this much concealer or highlighter. Good grief, we used to slather on some Noxzema, rinse it off, and walk out of the house looking like Jennifer Aniston (sort of).

My biggest problem, though, isn't that I need so many creams and serums to offset the signs of time. It's that I can't remember to do it all every day. I need alarms on my phone and strings on my fingers to help me remember the fish oil, my smoothie, and my makeup. Forgetfulness creates an awful lot of turbulence in life.

A few weeks ago I was scheduled to speak in our church on the same weekend my oldest son had his championship baseball tournament, and I was hosting a separate event for the church later in the day. I was determined to slay it all, to

---

[3] I keep saying I'll quit coloring my hair and go gray completely one day soon. I keep saying it, and yet I keep not doing it. Procrastination is the shield of fear and insecurity, I suppose.

not be incompetent like my refrigerator in any way.

I woke up that Sunday morning, grabbed my coffee, and spent some time reading my Bible. Then I fixed the kids some toast and juice and gave them instructions about proper church attire. My kids act as if they've never heard my spiel about not wearing ratty T-shirts with holes in them and that pajama pants are unacceptable in public. I explain every Sunday that we will not show up at church looking like the People of Walmart.[4]

Once I had reprogrammed everyone for the day, I took my shower, got dressed, and started doing my hair and makeup.

That's when all the children wanted to be in my room and bond with me as they retold *Peanuts* comic strips, discussed the batting averages of MLB players I'd never heard of, and analyzed every movie we'd ever seen as a family. I think one of them wanted to discuss the progression of United States foreign affairs from the Cold War to the present day and how that has affected the free market. Or maybe he just asked why I don't buy Pop-Tarts very often. I'm not sure.

All I wanted was to get my eyeliner on straight. I had a cat eye on the right side, but the left eye was more racoonish. I begged my children to leave so I could focus. They stared at me, motionless. Morgan kicked them out because he is a good husband, and also because I would be ministering God's Word later that morning, so hearing me shriek about eyeliner and the free market economy was a little scary for him.

I finished my hair and makeup in peaceful silence. Praise be to Jesus.

---

[4] Until I became a parent, I had no idea personal hygiene was a learned behavior and that I could produce humans with massive deficiencies in adhering to acceptable cultural standards of cleanliness.

We all rolled out the front door a little later. After I turned out of the neighborhood, a tragic realization crept from the back of my consciousness. *I forgot to put on concealer, foundation, and powder.*

I looked in the mirror, and there was my face, wearing some blush and heavy, caked-on eye makeup, but nothing else. There was nothing to cover and soften my charming laugh lines, the scars on my forehead, or my wicked awesome crow's-feet.

No big deal, right? I was going to be speaking on vulnerability and the courageous Christian life. My face could be a sermon illustration. No more masks! Real life! "How brave of her," everyone would say. I would reach heights of epic vulnerability in the Western world. Brené Brown could write a book about me.

Instead, I turned around and drove back home and slathered every bit of makeup I own on my face. Perhaps this seems shallow to you. Maybe you think this makeup of mine is akin to the duct tape that holds my refrigerator's ice dispenser in place. Perhaps it is a little bit. However, the simple truth is that I like how I look with my makeup, and although I am willing to be brave and vulnerable, I suppose I am also a little vain. It would have distracted me all morning, knowing I was walking around with a naked face. I wouldn't have felt courageous; I would have felt exposed.

Jesus said we would know a tree by its fruit. As I tap-tap-tapped the foundation under my wrinkly old lady eyes, only peace, love, and hope bloomed in my soul. I heard God laughing at me the same way I sometimes laugh when my kids do something that proves their unique quirkiness and slight immaturity. The makeup wasn't holding me together, and I knew it. God had bound me up in Himself, and it brought Him great joy to tease me a little about how I'd flubbed my morning.

Using duct tape or makeup isn't the root problem we face as humans. Just as the woman at the well would still need water every day of her life, we need physical things to help us function and cope. The battle we must fight is a spiritual one against the drive within us to look for salvation and rescue somewhere other than the Gospel. Surrendering to God is the only way forward.

Here's how another Bible version translates what Jesus told the woman at the well:

> "It's who you are and the way you live that count
> before God. Your worship must engage your spirit in
> the pursuit of truth. That's the kind of people the Father
> is out looking for: those who are simply and honestly
> themselves before him in their worship. God is sheer
> being itself—Spirit. Those who worship him must
> do it out of their very being, their spirits, their true
> selves, in adoration." (John 4:23–24 MSG)

What does this mean for you and for me, exactly? First, it means our success as Christians has nothing to do with developing a better version of ourselves. Second, it tells us that if we are thirsty and falling apart, what we need is to stand in God's presence and fully engage in worshipping Him with all we are and all we have.

THIRSTY WORSHIP

Lives of worship require us to march into the center of our neediness, scrape off all the tape, and chip away the glue that we've trusted to hold us together. Once we've set all that stuff aside, we can bring the full weight of our need for rescue into God's presence. Without our false ways of saving ourselves blocking us from Him, we can see who He really is as we raise our hands and say, "God, You know everything about me. You see the cracks and the broken places that scare me. They don't scare You, though. Right here, in this place where I am a mess and where my imperfection smacks of my incompetence, I choose to set aside my insecurity and lift my hands in surrender to You. Because, for some ridiculous reason, You chose me and You love me just as I am."

To worship God in truth, we will have to remember all the things that are most true about God *and* ourselves. I've already started a list for us, but feel free to add to it:

- We are limited (Psalm 103:15–16); God is infinite (Revelation 1:8).
- We are made in God's image (Genesis 1:27); God is love (1 John 4:16).
- We are His beloved children (1 John 3:1–2); He has adopted us into His family (Ephesians 1:5).
- God is a King who cares for the oppressed (Psalm 9:9; Luke 4:18–19; Revelation 19:16).
- God is a seeker of lost people (Luke 19:10) and a healer of broken souls (Psalm 147:3).
- God is like a mother hen who gathers her chicks under her wings (Luke 13:34).
- God is a Father who would send His Son into a dangerous place for the sake of saving those who could never save themselves (John 3:16; Romans 8:32; 1 John 4:9).

- God is a Brother who would willingly die so that His brothers and sisters could be reunited with their Father (Romans 8:29; Hebrews 2:10–15).
- God is a Spirit who comes as a helper and a comforter to empower us to live for the sake of something that is greater than ourselves (John 16:7; Romans 8:26–28; 1 Corinthians 12:4–11).

To worship God in spirit and in truth, we must kneel under the weight of our own need for salvation and rescue, hold out our hands, and receive whatever God offers us today—even if His provision doesn't make sense (kind of like using duct tape and a rag to repair a broken refrigerator). Sometimes worship looks like praying for a fractured friendship, blessing our enemies with baked goods, thanking God for even the bitter seasons of life, or embracing and owning our failures by accepting mercy and asking for a second chance.

Much about God is mysterious and hazy from a human perspective. I'm as skilled at understanding God as my refrigerator is at comprehending me. Somewhere inside that massive stainless steel box are electronic parts that are trying very hard to give me what I want. I know that if Old Silver were a sentient creature, she would want very much to reach her full potential. All the fixes and repairs are only temporary, though, because no refrigerator has eternal life. Eternal warranties do not exist in the world of appliances. The maker of that appliance will give you a year, just in case you get a lemon. After that, you and your pretty icebox are on your own.

That's not how it works with our Maker, however. He doesn't offer any warranties, because He doesn't make any lemons. He knows we all have some malfunctioning parts, and

He doesn't want us to try to fix them on our own. Refrigerators are temporal, *but we are eternal.* Our small attempts to hold ourselves together and save ourselves from all the broken parts of our souls will never quench our deepest thirst for the God who has a plan to repair this broken world—which is a good thing, since God longs to quench our thirst and invite us to join Him in the work.

Jesus told the Samaritan woman that facing the truth about her broken relationships was the key to finding the Messiah. Essentially, He was saying, "You need love, but no one will ever love you as I can." He wasn't offering her a better husband; He was presenting her a chance at transformation through a deep knowledge of who He was and what He would one day do on the cross.

Likewise, as we press into knowing Jesus and entrust Him with our imperfections and weaknesses, God's presence and power will transform us into God's holy people. But being made holy doesn't equate to being perfectly pure and obeying all the rules. After all, God called the Sabbath holy, and it never did a thing to raise itself above the other days of the week. God sets holy things apart because *He has a distinct purpose for them.* Likewise, Jesus has rescued you and made you holy because God's will is for you to be a fountain of living water. Any other kind of life will leave you parched and dry, thirsty for more.

Jesus didn't come to make us good enough. He came to tell us we could stop trying so hard and that we could *rest in His goodness.* There's not a tube of eye cream or a roll of tape in the whole universe that can come close to offering us what Jesus offers us.

"Come to Me, all you who labor and are heavy laden, and I will give you rest. Take My yoke upon you and learn from Me, for I am gentle and lowly in heart, and you will find rest for your souls. For My yoke is easy and My burden is light." (Matthew 11:28–30 NKJV)

The Samaritan woman came to a well for water, but in the end, she left her pot behind because of her life-changing encounter with Jesus. She ran back to her community and beckoned them all to come and meet a man she thought may be the Christ.

Meeting Jesus by a well or a refrigerator or in your car during rush hour can change you from a lonely soul who goes to get what she needs when no one is around into a person running toward your community with fresh hope and good news for the world.

God isn't looking for perfect people with massive influence who are confident and secure in every way. He's just looking for thirsty hearts that don't want to cover up their need any longer; He's looking for people who are ready to let Him fill their cup with His holiness.

In the following chapters, we will look at some of the specific ways we are often tempted to try to save ourselves and all the ways God has promised He is the best answer to our troubles. We will examine why God says we can be confident in who He is and how much He loves us. We will learn how amazing He already thinks we are—no hustle necessary. No matter how many pieces are falling off us today, Jesus is here to make all things new and to give us rest.

I only wish I could say the same about Old Silver. Because, seriously, the milk is about to drop through that crack.

CHAPTER 2

HOLY GUACAMOLE AND
LEGGINGS AS PANTS

How Your "Enoughness" Can't Save You

CHANCHO, WHEN YOU ARE A MAN, SOMETIMES YOU WEAR
STRETCHY PANTS IN YOUR ROOM. IT'S FOR FUN.
IGNACIO IN *NACHO LIBRE*

O nce upon a time, I met a boy in college. I hate how common and prosaic that sounds—as if I went to college to find a husband (I didn't). But that boy was the funniest, kindest boy I had ever met, and we became best friends during our sophomore year. He loved Jesus in profound and loyal ways that made my own faith seem a little flaky. I liked him a lot, but a few things were holding me back from falling madly in love, and I'm not just talking about the 1990s Christian culture rules about appropriate side-hugs.[5]

For starters, he had a girlfriend when we first met. She was super cute, and he just *knew* he would marry her. When they broke up, he was devastated; there was no way he wanted to go through that again. Lucky for him, I had totally kissed dating goodbye.[6]

---

[5] Sometimes when you think you're supposed to side-hug a person, he goes in for the regular kind of hug. Then his face is right up against your cheek, and your arm ends up pressed against the center of his torso, and all attempts at appropriateness are over. In my opinion, the best way to avoid embarrassing human contact like this is to just never leave your house. #notahugger

[6] I never read this somewhat controversial book that rocked youth groups in the late 1990s, but I was taught the principles and lived to tell about it. My family thought I had lost my mind, but even so, #jesuswasmyboyfriend #ikisseddatinggoodbye.

What I'm saying is that spiritually speaking, we didn't stand a chance. But there were some more earthly, natural barriers as well. This boy was a little shorter than I was, and I loved to wear heels. He also planned to enter vocational ministry after college, and I was throwing major deuces at raising my support as a university campus missionary. But every time this boy looked at me, I felt like I became a new person one molecule at a time. Despite having seen *When Harry Met Sally* 334 times, I decided we could be BFFs.

To make the friendship-only thing a little easier to maintain, I moved very far away and tried to find a taller boy—one with a non-church-related job who also looked at me with stars in his eyes.

After six years of looking, I realized there was no such boy in all the world. Around that time, I took a trip to Texas to visit my brother, and my heart fluttered as that previously friend-zoned boy and I shared a dinner. All the barriers became nonissues entirely. Right there, with a slice of margherita pizza in my hand, I was pleasantly surprised to discover I was in love with my best friend.

Thankfully, he felt the same way, and we were married a few months later.

I quit my job in the marketplace and tried to be a minister too. I never quite found my groove, though. In 1 Corinthians 9, Paul said to run our race to win the prize. But I ran my Campus Minister's Wife race a little more like Phoebe ran through Central Park in that episode of *Friends*, flailing about with her arms windmilling like a lunatic. I was awkward and not particularly skilled at ministry work. Then I got pregnant and found out that the least effective college ministry tactic is to have a pregnant woman pass out flyers for an outreach. I was off the hook. Sweet relief flooded my soul.

Having never quite figured out who I was after marriage and ministry wrecked my identity, I entered fully into the SAHM world. I birthed four babies in four and a half years. I highly recommend this pace of motherhood as a recipe for emotional disaster and a total loss of your sanity.

Even so, there is a lot I could say about the simplicity of motherhood as your full-time gig. It was the most beautiful thing that ever made me die a million deaths. To be an excellent stay-at-home parent, you really must learn to love those kids way more than things you always took for granted before having young children—such as your ability to sleep, the tautness of the skin on your stomach, and your entire arsenal of self-worth. Motherhood undid me, and I had nowhere to escape. I couldn't even hide in the bathroom, because those tiny people would bang on the door until I finally came out.

For a long time, I thought being a mom was the hardest thing I had ever done. Then we became pastors of a church. I had no clue what I was doing as a "pastor's wife," and it wasn't exactly my dream come true. Though I was used to my own flesh-and-blood children needing more than I could muster up most days, I soon learned that there are also *relatively specific expectations* put on pastors' wives. . .and I was not delivering.

According to the urban legends, as a "pastor's wife," I must be exceedingly sweet and submissive (emphasis on the word *submissive*). I probably play the piano or sing in the choir, but at the very least, I enjoy a rocking rendition of "Amazing Grace" by the praise band.[7] I *definitely* revere my husband as a near-godlike authority. I bake loaves of homemade bread for the poor weekly, and I am an impeccably wise and humble

---

[7] More cowbell, please.

mother. The pastor's wife always knows exactly what people expect from her and is capable of meeting those needs.

What's a girl to do when she realizes she doesn't have what everyone wants from her? Well, in my case, I mostly just freaked out and blamed my husband for choosing such a challenging career, because sometimes I'm mature like that.[8]

I don't know if you've ever had to admit you're less than legendary, but it's very humbling. Morgan told me one day I would have to be courageous and learn to be a leader. I wanted to shout at him, "I *did not ever* want to be a leader!" But instead, I just nodded and poured another cup of coffee, because I hate conflict—and besides, I knew he was right. God had set me up, tricked me into being a pastor's wife when I had never even meant to be in ministry at all. I was pretty sure I knew how Moses felt in front of that burning bush: wholly terrified and oddly bamboozled by the divine.

Moses' argument was that he wasn't good with words. Mine was that I was a coward and I didn't have enough faith for the PWL (pastor's wife life). I am not a person who naturally does "courageous" well. As a small child, I slept with my head under my covers for protection from scary sounds and bad guys. When I was eleven, I was the only one of all my cousins who understood how life-threatening it was to jump off the fifteen-foot-high dam into the lake near my grandparents' house. Even now, when I watch movies about some kind of massive, worldwide catastrophe, I always pity the people who survive the world apocalypse that has created a fractured and terrifying dystopian society. The people who never saw the

[8] Me: "Why did you become a pastor, anyway?" Him: "God told me to." Me: "That is no excuse." Him: "Yes, it is." Me: "We will have to agree to disagree." Him: "Your real problem is with God." Me: "That's none of your business." Him: [Massive eye roll.]

alien attack coming and are already with Jesus are the lucky ones, obviously.

Unfortunately, God didn't get my text message saying that if He ever needed a hero, He maybe shouldn't call on me.

THE WIND BENEATH MY WINGS

Despite my nonheroic nature, I do like superhero costumes. I'm a big fan of leggings in particular. I wear "sleep leggings" to bed. After I wake up, I put on my "workout leggings" to ensure I will be *forced* to work out (or at least feel very ashamed of my lack of discipline if I don't). Whether I make it to the gym or not (usually not), I change into my fancy leggings before dinner because my dignity requires this one thing of me. Then I put on new pajama leggings around nine thirty and call it a night.

I feel more capable and formidable in a good pair of leggings. Leggings for president, I say.

However, I once witnessed the potential dangers of the wrong pair of leggings. While I waited in line at the Target customer service desk, I noticed an *adorable* woman standing in front of me. Her outfit was on point. Cute sweater and boots, high ponytail, flawless makeup. Except there was one problem—and it wasn't the typical "wearing leggings as pants" problem that we have all bravely faced so many times. In a complete state of shock, I realized the woman was wearing *tights*. I could see her underwear *and her skin* through the fabric. I'm sure from the front they looked pantsish, but our backsides tend to stretch things out a little more. Her failed attempt to cover up a part of her that shouldn't be seen was right there, in full view.

This display of true humanity brought to mind my own failure at figuring out how to cover my not-enoughness. All my attempts to hide my lack of faith and courage so I could appear to know what I was doing were failing. I was vulnerable, out in public, with my existential underwear on full display.

I needed the same kind of help my Target buddy required. We all really need the help of a friend who will pull us aside and tell us our leggings will never be thick enough to cover our not-enoughness.

We need the Holy Spirit to send a Ryan Gosling–like person to knock on our door and gently break it to us: "Hey, girl, you're trying too hard here. You're expecting too much out of yourself. Maybe hide a little deeper in who God is and let Him cover all the places where you're too thinned out."

Of course, accepting criticism and correction is always less humbling and humiliating in theory than it is in practice. When my husband tried to be my Ryan Gosling, suggesting I "learn to be a leader," I wanted to set fire to his words and use them to burn down the house. But I didn't, of course. I just let them sit near me, a little candle of proof in the middle of the dark reality that I was in over my head in life. I waited for God to show me if Morgan was right, that I was actually capable of growing into the kind of person who wasn't so afraid she was less than people needed her to be.

I hate waiting, don't you?

Waiting for God to show up proves how powerless we are. And yet faith requires we sit in the story of how we are not enough without Him and remain expectant of His goodness. God seems to hold mystery as one of His crowning glories.

If you ask me, God is a little strange in that way.

But in Ecclesiastes 11:5–6, Solomon wrote that even

though God's miraculous power is mysterious, our responsibility to be faithful in our daily life need not puzzle us. Get up, do your work, grow stronger, smarter, wiser, braver, and God will show up at some point. As for me, I threw myself into the work of the PWL and hoped God would block everyone's view of my paper-thin leggings.

So there I was, up to my eyebrows in pastoral appointments, speaking engagements, dishes, laundry, writing assignments, taxiing kids to activities, and cooking healthy(ish) dinners. Somewhere in the middle of trying to be a wife, mom, writer, and pastor's wife, I lost my grasp on my own identity. The unraveling of my identity that had begun with falling in love with my best friend ended in me trying to be everything everyone needed me to be and forgetting who God had made me to be. I had lost my connection to God as my source of living water.

Thankfully, waiting for God can be discombobulating and reorienting all at the same time.

One day, I slipped on a pair of leggings to meet my friend Quinn at a Tex-Mex restaurant. There, God finally showed up.

HOLY GUACAMOLE

Quinn asked me a doozy of a question in that restaurant: "What's it really like to be a pastor's wife?"[9]

I didn't want to scare her with too much honesty, so I spent a minute thinking about how best to respond. I stared at my plate, with its empty queso bowl and the big gap where enchiladas once sat. Only the obligatory serving of rice and beans

---

[9] Making space for other people's stories is so important. I am grateful that we have friends who allow us to be vulnerable and honest about what we're going through. It's a gift. That said, I cried a lot during this next portion of the story. I'm not sure Quinn was prepared for that. You get what you get in friendship sometimes.

remained. I noticed Quinn's plate still had rice and beans on it too. A quick glance around at the other tables revealed that almost every abandoned dish still had rice and beans. The truth hit me like a mariachi band.

"Being married to a pastor is like being the rice and beans on a plate of Tex-Mex. Nobody ordered me; I just came with my husband when they hired him. Everyone expects me to be there and to meet their personal needs, but no one is surprised if I'm not all that amazing in general. They just hope I'm not terrible, you know?"

Saying these words felt like a confession, as if I had at last been allowed to tell the truth about how thin my leggings were and how scared I was of never finding a way to be more than overstretched and left over.

Quinn looked at me with faithful eyes and spoke a blessing: "But you're not rice and beans. You're *tableside guacamole*."

I love you forever, Quinn Smith.[10]

Friendship and kindness often stretch to cover us until our souls catch up with God's truth about who we are. A good friend reminds us that what we feel about ourselves is not always the truth. What Quinn blessed me with that day was a universal truth about all of God's children. What's true about me is also true about you.

You are not left over. You are not an extra person who was served up and must be scooted aside so that everyone can reach the queso better. You are unique and beautiful, a gift to the world that God is preparing for many, many great works. He has put the full measure of the Holy Spirit inside you. You are made holy and precious by the loving sacrifice of Jesus.

---

[10] Quinn is practically a saint. She not only is wise and encouraging, but she is also a justice seeker who works tirelessly to help end human trafficking with her business, Remnant Studios. I wish you all could know her.

Don't be afraid. Savor the Word of God, written so that you would know the truth and so that the truth would set you free. Soak in the presence of God, which is always with you, singing over you with songs of joy and deliverance.

There are no obligatory side dishes in the Kingdom of God. We are all holy tableside guacamole. We're prepared fresh daily in Christ, with new mercies every morning. Should we fail to fully live out the love God has put in us today, He'll save us from our distress. If the day offers us bad news, we can cling to the hope that what our enemy has meant for evil, God intends for good. Failure is never our final destiny in Jesus.

While it's true we are not enough on our own, Jesus becomes enough for us every time we fall short. We miss the great gift of God's grace when we try to save ourselves from our lack of enoughness. Our social media feeds, books, and podcasts are full of the narrative "I am strong and powerful and can't be stopped. No one can tell me what to do. Forget anyone who gets in the way of my happiness." It's understandable, really. Outside the church, with no Gospel to give them hope, people are left with no option except to champion themselves.

But in Christ, we find we have a unique kind of champion with a unique strategy for winning in life.

BLESS YOUR HEART

As God's children, we are called to a peculiarly different standard of spiritual. Jesus once declared, "Blessed are the poor in spirit, for theirs is the kingdom of heaven" (Matthew 5:3 ESV).

The first time I read Matthew 5, I thought maybe Jesus was kidding. Was He winking as He rattled off the Beatitudes during this Sermon on the Mount, but the disciples just didn't include that detail in their account? *"LOL, Jesus, we should be poor in spirit so we can inherit heaven. Good one!"*

However, here in Texas, blessing people for being a mess is a way of life.

Bless.

Bless it.

Bless him, Lord.

And the coup de grâce of all southern blessings: *Bless your heart.*

How many times in the past twenty years have I heard blessings flung upon people discovered to be in dubious circumstances? The current tally is one bazillion twenty-nine. Growing up in Southern California, I never once heard someone's heart blessed. If people were hot messes, we just sort of ignored that as long as their drama didn't directly affect us. We suggested a day at the beach, a night out with friends, or, in dire cases, some kind of herbal supplement that might ease the suffering. We did not bless their hearts.

It took me a while to figure out what "Bless your heart" actually means.

At first I thought it was a sneaky way to insult someone and still sound kind. Like pity with a razor-sharp edge of judgment. While "Bless so-and-so's heart" is unfortunately used that way sometimes, I've learned that the expression is also part of a cultural commitment to empathy. Blessing the hearts of others makes space for the lack and poverty we all face as limited and flawed human beings, which is what Jesus was really getting at in Matthew 5. Once we admit we're spiritually incompetent without Him, we can genuinely inherit the Kingdom of Heaven.

If we're poor in spirit, we know there's nothing we can do

to get our cosmic leggings to stretch adequately over our sin. God gave us the Bible as a mirror to show us the flimsiness of our attempts to save ourselves. He also gave us one another, because it's really not good for us to be alone.

Ideally, life in God's kingdom looks something like a community of love: We all love God, and we all love one another more than ourselves. We use our talents to bless one another. We always believe the best about others and keep the intentions of our hearts toward them pure in God's sight. We humbly acknowledge our weaknesses, and we strengthen others through prayer and encouragement. We cheer when someone else has a victory. We dance at weddings. We grieve when others lose, comforting them with our loyalty and understanding. We mourn when death separates us from the people we love, even though we know it isn't a permanent loss.

Unfortunately, life is rarely like that on a grand scale. It's more like this: We love God a lot, but maybe not always as much as our current attempts to quiet the ache of our souls with comfort, achievement, or some other distraction. We try really hard to love others, but some people make that really hard for us. To compensate, we avoid them whenever possible and focus on the people who are less complicated to love. We acknowledge our weaknesses when pressed, but mostly we try to ignore them and hope no one notices. We cheer when others have victories that don't wound our own pride or make us feel insecure. We dance at weddings if we like the music. We grieve when others lose, but we also experience desperate gratitude that *it isn't us this time*. We mourn when death separates us from the people we love, and we wish we had been a little more honest, a little more vulnerable, or had taken a bit more time to tell them how much they really meant to us. We are deeply grateful that eternity will clear up a lot of the angst swirling in our hearts.

We're all standing in a cosmic Target, using our inadequate leggings to cover the fear that we're unwanted, not enough, extra rice and beans. Jesus is in line beside us, though, and He's holding out a bag that has a better outfit in it. He wants to do more than cover up our shameful attempts at self-salvation. Jesus wants to array us in His holiness. But how do we turn and receive that bag, exactly?

SAY YES TO THE DRESS

Years ago, before we were pastors, a leader Morgan respected asked him how his campus ministry was going. In all honesty, it was going great. Over fifty students had committed their lives to Christ that semester. Several were planning to enter vocational ministry. All of them were sharing their faith with their friends and were excited about Jesus. Morgan explained this to the respected leader, using the word "phenomenal" in his description.

This leader didn't agree with Morgan's assessment. His words thinned my husband out a little abruptly.

"That's not phenomenal. Phenomenal would be filling several thousand seats in the basketball arena for your weekly meeting. You shouldn't use that word ever again," the leader said.

After processing this terrible blow to his confidence, Morgan found that, in a way, the man was right. By our "bigger is better" earthly definition of success, a stadium full of disciples *would* seem phenomenally better than what God was doing in our campus ministry.

But Jesus never said bigger is better. He actually said the exact opposite.

What felt like an attack on my husband's ability as a leader was really ignorance of God's kingdom ways. The man's words were meant to shame my husband, but they ended up being a reminder of how precious humility can be. Once we accept how weak and small we are and submit to God's sovereign will, we no longer have to live up to the world's exaggerated expectations of us. Insinuations and insults become blessings in God's kingdom.

Consider these words of Jesus:

"Blessed are you when people insult you, persecute you and falsely say all kinds of evil against you because of me. Rejoice and be glad, because great is your reward in heaven, for in the same way they persecuted the prophets who were before you." (Matthew 5:11–12 NIV)

The phenomenal news in Matthew 5 is that we get a reward one day. The not-so-phenomenal news is that we may be treated worse than unwanted rice and beans in the meantime. Rejoice anyway, Jesus encouraged us.

Rejoicing can be an act of obedience, which Jesus defined as loving Him. Likewise, John 14 says that if we love Jesus, we will obey His commands. I'm always a little afraid when God tells me to obey and follow Him, because I know the story of the rich kid in Luke 18. It goes something like this:

A rich and powerful young man came to Jesus asking what good thing he could do to inherit eternal life. Jesus replied that doing so was easy—he just needed to keep all the commandments. Impressively, the young man said he had already done that. *Check that one off, Jesus!* But Jesus told him there was one thing he still lacked: "Sell everything you have and give to the poor, and you will have treasure in heaven. Then come, follow me" (v. 22 NIV). The wealthy kid walked away saddened at the thought of losing so much.

I've never fully understood what that young man expected from Jesus that day. I've always imagined him as a know-it-all. Maybe this guy knew he'd kept all the commandments, and he wanted a gold star for his awesomeness. Perhaps Jesus saw his diligent heart and knew that if he could risk so much to become a disciple, he would find rest at last in the Gospel. We find here a very modern character in the ancient world. He wanted to *do* something to save himself because all his success and comfort were not enough to satisfy his soul.

To find eternal life, the man would have had to change everything about his earthly life. Jesus wasn't saying the man had been wrong to keep the commandments perfectly in the past. He wasn't shaming him or trying to make the man feel guilty. Jesus wasn't saying that his being wealthy was inherently evil. He was telling this man that losing everything that could never save him was the quickest way to find what really mattered.

When the required sacrifice saddened the young man, Jesus said cramming a camel through the eye of a needle would be easier than trying to hold on to earthly wealth *and* gain eternal life through personal strength. But He also said that, as impossible as it seemed, nothing is impossible for God.

Jesus and my husband and Quinn had already told me everything I needed to know. To be the person God made me to be, I would have to pass through the eye of a needle and leave behind all the ways I was trying to save myself with my own abilities and talents. If Jesus is asking us to do the impossible today, He's also ready to provide a way through. But obedience will require we let some things go and pick up a new way of living.

WHAT'S IN YOUR HANDS

I left that Tex-Mex restaurant sad to know I had been so wrong about so many things. The story of the rich young man gave me hope, though, because the Bible doesn't say he *didn't* sell his possessions and come back. It only tells us he left sad, feeling the weight of the loss of so many blessings. Maybe that young ruler sold everything and followed Jesus. Maybe one night around the campfire with the other disciples, he heard the story of the loaves and fishes from Mark 6. Perhaps he heard about how Jesus looked at a measly offering of food for thousands of people and blessed it:

> *Taking the five loaves and the two fish and looking up*
> *to heaven, he gave thanks and broke the loaves. Then*
> *he gave them to his disciples to distribute to the people.*
> *(Mark 6:41 NIV)*

The word for "thanks" here in Greek is *eulogeo*, which means to praise, give thanks to, speak well of, extol, or bless. It's used many times in the New Testament, like when Jesus blessed and broke the bread at the last supper and when He appeared to the disciples after He had risen. Jesus ascended to heaven after giving the disciples a eulogeo blessing.

Eulogeo is what Jesus does when He sees a small offering that can become great in His kingdom.

God knows no scarcity, after all. He is abundant provision. Jesus can pass out your not-enough and feed the hungry masses. He looks at the leggings that barely cover your bum and asks you to stretch until you're sure you can't stretch one millimeter more, and then He blows your mind and makes the impossibility of full coverage into a reality.

And this changes everything. Because you and I and that used-to-be rich young man are all more than a pair of leggings or broken bread in the hands of Jesus. We're more than Holy Guacamole for the hungry. We're much more than camels squeezing through tight spaces. These are all just metaphors and parables to help us understand the greatest miracle God has done despite our inherent not-enoughness: we were made to belong to God as His beloved people.

We have been loved enough to draw the Son of God out of heaven, down to earth, to live and to die so we can be united with God forever. He will love us to the very end (John 13:1), and nothing will ever be able to take that away from us. His love is the absolute and guaranteed reward for the girl who doesn't want to fall in love with a certain boy, for the mom with too many little kids, for the person who doesn't know how to be a good leader, for the rich young ruler and the poor young follower.

Go ahead, put on your stretchy pants and find your best life in God as His Holy Guacamole. He is a more-than-enough hero to save us all. No alien invasion or world apocalypse necessary.

CHAPTER 3

Sit Down, Deborah

How Quitting Can't Save You

For several years of my early childhood, I knew exactly what I wanted to be when I grew up. In a stroke of predictability, I added up my love of pink, tutus, and attention and decided being a ballerina was my future calling. I was confident that I would grow up and set the stage on fire with my grace and beauty. Spoiler alert: I am not dancing in *The Nutcracker* this Christmas at a theater near you. Nor do I ever dance anywhere except the privacy of my own kitchen, should Spotify suddenly bless me by streaming Steve Perry's "Oh Sherrie" or Whitney Houston's "I Wanna Dance with Somebody" while I wait for pasta to boil.

But back when I was five years old, my parents signed me up for ballet lessons because they couldn't say no to my cuteness (they also didn't know my drive to dance required a spatula in my hand to really kick in). Five-year-old Carrie was thrilled the first day of class. I donned my leotard and arrived ready to enter into greatness, one pointed toe at a time. Week after week, I worked to become the great dancer I was meant to be. Then sometime around Christmas, we took a break from classes for the holiday season.

I was appalled. We had been tricked and bamboozled by our lovely teacher. There had not been a single show yet! When would we get to perform? When would all this hard work be proven useful? We owed it to the public to bless them with a performance. We owed it to our egos to be the graceful centers of attention we were meant to be!

So great was the offense that I quit ballet. My parents then signed me up for soccer. I was pretty good at that, actually. I played for the following ten years of my life.

As my childhood progressed, I would regret my decision to quit ballet. The dream of being a ballerina never entirely went away, even as I excelled as an athlete. I don't think I missed some calling to ballet or the stage, but I always knew in my heart that I'd quit for the wrong reasons. I'd quit to save myself from disappointment.

At the age of five, I was too young to predict that quitting would become my first line of defense when circumstances became more challenging than I wanted them to be. What began as a five-year-old's childish temper tantrum developed over the years into a well-practiced art of taking my ball and going home. I've had to learn to distrust myself when something deep inside me shouts, "That's it! I quit! Peace out, my friends!"

My quitter voice is not to be trusted.

What does the voice in your head shout at you when life doesn't go quite the way you want? If you aren't sure, it could be you need to listen a little more carefully. When conflict arises, do you rush into the fight with your proverbial guns blazing? Do you take a minute to assess the most strategic way to end or defuse the argument? Or do you make like Forrest Gump and just start running? I bet in most basic life scenarios, you tend to show up predisposed to a specific, consistent re-action if you don't actively choose a different one. There isn't a "right" or "wrong" way to respond to conflict, but the outcome generally favors the people who let wisdom—not their emotions—guide their actions. Accessing and applying that wisdom, though, requires a lot of hard work in our heads and our hearts.

HERO WORK

Courage comes in many forms, and in my case, it's mostly a willingness to suffer silently and then enter eternity. So you can imagine my shock and surprise when I went to see *Wonder Woman* a few years ago, and upon witnessing the titular character fight her way across No Man's Land, I sat forward in my seat, gripped the armrests, and allowed every voice inside me to shout: "I want to do *that*. Put me in the fight!"

I had previously assumed my young sons pretending to be Spider-Man and Batman was the same kind of play I'd enjoyed as a child when I pretended to be a ballerina. But there in that theater, I knew different. The longing my sons had wasn't to be Spider-Man; it was a longing to beat the unbeatable opponent, to win the unwinnable fight, and to save a world of people incapable of saving themselves.

Wonder Woman showed me that hero work is at the center of all the things I love best about Gospel work.

Unfortunately, for the most part, women have been side-lined in these kinds of quests in church history. We've been the ones behind the scenes—the helpers, the cheerleaders. That has begun to change in many places, for which I am incredibly grateful. But, as the saying goes, we have to "see it so we can be it." I guess that was what happened to me in the movie theater that day. I saw a woman being courageous and going where no one else was capable of going, fighting with strengths and talents that were unique to her, and accomplishing something incredible. She made me want to be a warrior who refuses to quit.

I'm not entirely sure why it has taken me so long to get here. From the very creation of woman, God has called her a warrior. In Genesis 2:18, God made the woman and called her man's "*ezer*." Although many Bible versions translate it as "helper" or "helpmeet," the writers of the Old Testament used this word often in a military context to mean "strong helper." It certainly does not mean "helper" in all things domestic or ordinary; it means something much closer to "warrior" or "defense." Ezer is a name used for God Himself as Israel's strong defense (Exodus 18:4; Deuteronomy 33:7, 26, 29; Psalms 20:2; 33:20; 70:5; 115:9, 10, 11; 121:1–2; 124:8; 146:5; Hosea 13:9). Genesis 1:27 says that God created man and woman in His image. Then Genesis 2:18 tells us God made women to reflect His divine, heroic, rescuing nature as an "ezer."

So when my insecurities and fear rise and clearly command me to give up, sit down, and find a safe place in the back seat, I remind myself that I'm a warrior woman, made to be a strong defense, armed with uniquely female weapons to fight alongside the men of the world. If men have struggled to carry the weight of leadership in history, could it be that this has been, in part, because the women around them haven't been empowered to help them as members of the frontline defense? Perhaps, in order to lead better, the men of the world have needed the uniquely female, fiercely devoted defenders God intended them to have alongside them.

Beyond a fictional woman from the island of Themyscira, some biblical women can inspire us with their effectiveness, strength, and refusal to quit.

In particular, I'm thinking of Deborah.

HELLO, DEBORAH

This is how the Bible introduces us to Deborah: "Now Deborah, a prophetess, the wife of Lappidoth, was judging Israel at that time. She used to sit under the palm of Deborah between Ramah and Bethel in the hill country of Ephraim, and the people of Israel came up to her for judgment" (Judges 4:4–5 ESV).

There is no ancient asterisk after this introduction. In fact, the narrator has left Deborah's life up until this moment unexplained entirely. The writer of Judges[11] did not tell us that Deborah was promoted to the highest leadership position in Israel because no men were available that year. She was not a prophet because of some weird life circumstance that forced the people of Israel to lower their standards and accept a woman as a leader in matters of religion and ethics. The text doesn't say that her husband's position allowed her to be an exception to the general rule that women should really stay home and cook and have babies.

Despite all this, I have heard Deborah's story told as a kind of cautionary tale: "Be careful, men—if you don't lead well, then God may have to use a woman." After all, these teachers have told us, desperate times call for drastic measures.

Nonsense and hogwash. While God includes us in His plans, He is not "desperate" for any man or woman's help. He

---

[11] While the book of Judges itself doesn't indicate who wrote it, the Talmud attributes it to the prophet Samuel.

doesn't use anyone He doesn't explicitly call. To say God will only use women out of desperation douses any fire that may be burning in a woman's heart to make a difference in the world by becoming the ezer she is destined to be. It also dishonors Deborah's contribution to her people by making it seem as if she was less than worthy of respect as a leader.

Explaining away Deborah's leadership is a tragedy and weakens our women as individuals and our communities at large. Let's just let Deborah be who she was, a judge and a prophetess who was called by God to do something incredibly important. And what was it she did, exactly?

DEBBIE NOT SO DOWNER

In Judges 4 and 5, we can read the story of how Deborah sent for Barak and told him God was sending him to fight Sisera, the commander of the Canaanite army. The Israelites had been violently oppressed by Sisera for twenty years. Judges 5 shows us that Sisera's treatment of the Israelites was cruel and included the trafficking of women. He was well-armed with chariots made of iron, which were unbeatable weapons of mass destruction at that time. The battle Deborah told Barak to fight was unwinnable. Even so, Barak said he would go. But he asked Deborah to go with him. She agreed and informed Barak the glory of the victory would be given to a woman and not to him, because he chose not to go alone.

Once Barak and Deborah led ten thousand soldiers to the battle site, Deborah called for Barak to charge into battle at a precise moment, assuring him that God had gone before him. He obeyed her, and just as the action began, heavy rain rolled in, rendering the enemies' chariots useless. The result of the ensuing victory was forty years of peace for Israel. Judges 5 depicts Deborah and Barak singing together about the victory and their gratitude to God for leading them and rescuing them.

Now, the same people who say Deborah was a fluke may also tell you that Barak was a coward for being a man who was afraid to go to battle without a woman by his side, and that his "punishment" for cowardice was losing the glory of the victory to a woman. However, Deborah never used the word *punishment* or *consequence*. She merely said, "Nevertheless, the road on which you are going will not lead to your glory, for the LORD will sell Sisera into the hand of a woman" (Judges 4:9 ESV). It's possible we have read Deborah's prophetic statement about Barak's future as a punishment because we have accepted an unbiblical view of men and women in general, namely, that men should always be given credit and glory. Subconsciously, we may even believe women aren't meant to display God's glory in the earth by courageously fighting for God's people alongside men.

The courage of Barak, as well as God's general affirmation of his character and actions in Judges 4, is proven by the only other place Barak's name appears in the scriptures. Hebrews 11:32–34 lists Barak among our heroes of faith:

> *For time would fail me to tell of Gideon, Barak, Samson, Jephthah, of David and Samuel and the prophets— who through faith conquered kingdoms, enforced justice, obtained promises, stopped the mouths of lions, quenched the power of fire, escaped the edge of the sword, were made strong out of weakness, became mighty in war, put foreign armies to flight. (ESV)*

Barak asked Deborah to go with him. But instead of assuming that's a sign of weakness, could we ponder the possibility that Barak caught a glimpse of the glory of a true ezer in Deborah? He saw the warrior-defender God made her to be, the active help she alone could offer, and he knew he didn't want to fight without her aid. Could it be that Barak was humble and asked for Deborah's help because he realized that he and Deborah would accomplish more together than Barak could on his own? How much faith would it require for a man of that culture and time to command ten thousand men with a woman beside him, alerting him to the exact moment he should charge into battle?

In all honesty, Barak probably needed the same amount of faith we need today to embrace new strategies and perspectives that make space for women and men to lead side by side. Barak needed enough faith to realize this battle wasn't his chance to prove he was a singularly unbeatable hero; rather, it was an opportunity to be one part of God's plan to rescue His people. He needed enough faith in God to turn away from his culture's patriarchal teachings about gender, shame, and honor and faithfully fulfill his role as a leader alongside another anointed leader who happened to be female.

And what about Deborah? The Bible makes it sound so simple in Judges 4:9, telling us Deborah "arose" (ESV). But surely she did more than just get up and head to a battle?

The Hebrew word for "arose" here is *quwm*. It is a word of action, meaning to rise up so as to become powerful, to accomplish, or to establish. *Quwm* is used many, many times in the Old Testament, and it is always used in connection with a precise, intense moment of purpose and action. It is the word that describes the way God made His covenant with

Abraham; *quwm* describes the way Hannah arose to ask the Lord for a child; and *quwm* is the kind of rescue the psalmist asked for again and again from God.

Deborah didn't just stand up. Deborah got up and got to work, serving Israel with wisdom and strength alongside Barak.

Perhaps you're thinking now, *But I'm no Deborah. I'm not a prophet. People don't come to me to ask me for wisdom or for righteous judgment, and I'm certainly not commanding an army.*

Who told you that? What has happened since the days of your childhood, when stories of rescue and adventure drew you into books and movies? When did you forget all the times you lay in bed as a child and imagined saving the last dolphin in the world or discovering you could fly, which meant the president needed you to help rescue people in distress? What happened to the dreams of your youth—the ones that involved inventing a car that never needed fuel or discovering a cure for cancer? What or whom did you dream of rescuing as a child? A parent in distress? An old run-down house at the end of a road? A sibling or friend who was being bullied? All the lost puppies in the world?

Do you ever wonder if those things and people are still waiting for you to fight to save them?

Did you *decide* to sit down one day and forget to arise again? Or did someone or something knock you down and convince you that you ought to stay down?

I know what happened to me. Motherhood laid me out flat. I entered survival mode, and the smallness of my life tricked me into quitting all my bigger dreams for a little while. I forgot about the little girl I once was, who dreamed of being all sorts of things: a ballerina, an artist, a lawyer, an environmental activist who would clean up the oceans so every beach would be pristine. I forgot about the twenty-year-old I once was, who chased her dream of working in Hollywood and making beautiful films that could inspire the world to live a better story. I even forgot about the twenty-five-year-old woman I once was, who dreamed of creating a life with the man she loved, in which both of them lived out their courageous faith and watched God's dreams unfold before them.

It took a little work and a lot of help from trusted people in my life, but eventually, I arose. If you're lying flat on your back somewhere, or just reluctantly hiding away from a battle you know God has called you to fight, have you asked yourself what could happen if you arose as Deborah did?

On the day God meets you on that battlefield and secures the victory for you, what will your song of victory be? How can you add your voice to the song God is already singing over you and in the world?

A NEW SONG

My friend Wendell preached about songs in church one day. He spoke about the song of the next generation and the need young people have for older generations to teach them their songs. At the beginning of his sermon, he asked us to think of what we would choose as our own personal theme song if our lives were a movie—the song that would play if we walked into an important room. He asked for a few volunteers to stand up and share their picks.

The people of our church played along. One woman stood and sang a few lines from "Amazing Grace." Another dazzled us by singing lyrics proclaiming our inherent value to God.

It was such a beautiful moment.

As everyone had apparently chosen songs about *Jesus*, I sat silently in the front row beside my pastor/husband, because I was pretty sure I hadn't understood the assignment. I had been trying to pick between Run DMC's "It's Tricky" and the Commodores' "Brick House," and now those songs seemed awfully, well. . .*worldly* compared to everyone else's. But in my defense, my life really does feel tricky most days, and I really do long to be "mighty, mighty."[12]

Now, if I had been thinking about Barak and Deborah when Wendell asked that question, I probably would have answered differently. If I had remembered the song they sang together in Judges 5 about the might and strength of their enemy, the impossibility of the battle, the glorious arrival of God's holy rescue, and the extraordinary way God allowed them to arise and join in with what He was doing that day, I would have sung a whole different song. I'm not entirely sure what song I would have selected, though, because it seems like a weighty choice.

Biblical songs like Barak and Deborah's are rare and always point to an incredibly important moment in God's story. Adam sang out of joy in the garden when God created woman. Hannah sang a song of praise to God when Samuel was born. Mary sang after the angel told her she would birth the Messiah. And Barak and Deborah sang when a man and a woman arose and led together in submission to God and to one another's giftings.

All of them were stopping amid God's blessing to give Him praise and acknowledge the miracle God had done for them.

---

[12] I often mention in passing that I have had a hard time finding my lane as a pastor's wife. I think this anecdote is one that explains how that actually plays out. #whatisafirstladyreallylike #pastorswifelife

The contemporary world is moving at breakneck speed. Do we remember to stop and sing our own songs of praise when God proves His faithfulness? Perhaps our inclination to quit is connected to the unyielding pace of life that beats us up and knocks us down again and again. We quickly forget we are part of God's greater story—his Holy Guacamole—and that He sings with gusto and joy over us all the time. Zephaniah 3:17 (ESV) says: "The LORD your God is in your midst, a mighty one who will save; he will rejoice over you with gladness; he will quiet you by his love; he will exult over you with loud singing."

I would like to think God is singing over me with a singer/songwriter brilliance mixed with the depth of a slow jam/spoken word. But for all I know, some days He could be making spa music using whale sounds and a pan flute because I am so chill He can't even deal. The problem is, I often miss His song altogether because it is so loud down here on planet earth. We live in constant noise. There is the rattle and hum of my responsibilities, the sound of my family's needs, the texts from friends, the endless notifications on my phone, the noise of all the voices of the past trying to keep me afraid of obeying God today, and the many voices of fear about what tomorrow may hold.

To learn to hear the song of God over our lives, we must develop disciplines that drive out the voices and songs that aren't God's. Listening is a skill we can't develop without practicing it. We need to find a quiet place to sit and teach our souls to hear God's song above the din of life.

A QUIET PLACE

A few years ago I began practicing contemplative prayer as a part of my morning routine. I started waking up in the dark morning hours before the rest of our house bustled with the ever-present need of Mom. I sat on the sofa with a twenty-minute timer on my phone and waited in the silence. I chose a word that felt meaningful each day, like "peace" or "Jesus" or "quiet," and I pressed every thought out of my mind with this word. I trusted that Zephaniah 3:17 was true and God was in my midst. I let my longing to experience the song He was singing bring a stillness to my body, and I just. . .sat.

I did not experience some kind of mystical angelic visitation.

I did not hear the audible voice of God.

I did not learn any new brilliant fact about God.

What I did find there in the stillness and silence was peace. I was suddenly aware that the frenetic way we live our lives is breaking down our spiritual grit and discipline. We are connected to everyone we know (and so many we don't know) by technology. Yet we're disconnected from ourselves in many ways and disconnected from God in many more. But there on my sofa, while my dog lay at my feet and my family lay in bed dreaming, I heard something in all the nothing. I heard that there is more of God's power and love in me than I often realize. I heard that a silent God is not an ambivalent God. I listened to the promise that waiting for Him is a kind of reward in and of itself. Most of all I heard my soul exhale with relief as it remembered that God has a plan and that nothing can ever separate me from His love.

It's strange, the way spiritual things work. In silence, we can hear. In weakness, we find God's strength. In generosity, we receive His blessing. In service to others, He meets our needs. In death, God lavishes us with eternal life.

I have come to believe it is actually impossible to really

quit. We can try to run away from God and His will, but like someone caught in a sci-fi time warp, we will run smack into God and His will again and again until we finally give up on quitting and run, at long last, straight to God.

Who has God made you to be? What do you truly want in life? Who has God called you to walk alongside? I found the answers to those questions by sitting in the silence. I have come to accept that who I am is not always who people think I am. Who I am is not even always who I think I am. What I am capable of achieving is sometimes more than I expect from myself, but anytime life and God require more than I can muster, God is always capable of making up the difference.

To make any progress in life, though, we first must arise. And some of us need to preach that to ourselves with a little more gusto.

PREACH, GIRL

Last week, Morgan and I traveled to Nashville to take a three-day preaching class with some other pastors. I usually wouldn't have signed up for the class because traveling amid school and kids' activities requires extensive organizational miracles that overwhelm me. I have to arrange for places for my kids to sleep, rides to and from school, meals, practice schedules, and game schedules, and I have to enlist some brave person to do my daughter's hair for her ballet classes. However, one of our favorite leaders and friends called and encouraged me to come. So I did.

I was one of only four women in the class.

If you have never experienced being an "only" in a room, then the next part of this chapter may be hard to understand.

While I knew I was wanted and accepted in that room, I struggled to feel comfortable. My soul was on edge, never wholly able to relax. My vulnerability was heightened by the fact that for generations, women have been excluded from the pulpit in most places. What's more, I was nervous because I would have to preach a message before an assessment team on the last day of the class.

But on that day, I arose. I stood there and told five men about childbirth and Romans 8, and how the pain we endure in life is often just birth pangs passing through us as God births His love in new ways. I told them funny stories about birthing babies, and I admitted that I had failed many times to press into the contractions with the people I love, but that God was helping me learn not to turn away from the hard circumstances we face.

When I was finished and the assessment began, every man had the same encouragement for me: "Preach with more authority."

I am a fortunate woman to be called upon by men of authority to walk in more authority. In many ways, these men were Deborahs in my life that day. They were pointing at a battlefield and telling me God had called me to fight. Countless women have been discouraged from positions of authority because of Paul's instructions for the church of Ephesus in 1 Timothy 2:12: "I do not permit a woman to teach or to exercise authority over a man; rather, she is to remain quiet" (ESV). These women are never pointed to Junia, a woman leader in the early church (Romans 16:7); to Priscilla, whom, along with her husband, Aquila, we find teaching in the church in Acts 18; or to the women who prophesied in the early church in Acts 21 and 1 Corinthians 11.

So what's really going on in 1 Timothy 2?

Timothy faced a unique situation in Ephesus, and Paul addressed that in this verse. The women in the church were illiterate and uneducated but the product of a culture that worshipped goddesses and apparently allowed all sorts of disrespectful and prideful behavior in its women. The word for "authority" used in 1 Timothy 2:12 is the Greek word *autheteo*, and as Dr. Dave Ward points out in his sermon "The Church, the Truth, and Women in Ministry,"[1] *autheteo* is not the word used for "authority" anywhere else in the New Testament. *Autheteo* means to thrust oneself out into a situation. It implies the women in this church were interrupting the teaching in the church and rudely correcting their husbands, who were more educated and knowledgeable than they were. Also, Ward points out that by saying "I do not permit" instead of something more permanent like "It is not permitted," Paul used language that doesn't imply a general rule for all women. This verse should not be used to bar women from places of authority, particularly because Paul affirms women as leaders in other letters. If we take a wider lens and look at the Bible as a whole, we find a great deal of evidence that leads us to believe that men and women were created by God to walk side by side, in submission to one another, as leaders in the world and lovers of God.

To lead courageously and effectively, men and women need each other more than we have been taught. I saw so clearly in that preaching class that I will never become the woman God made me to be without the help and friendship of the men God has placed in my life. Likewise, as I offered these men my own thoughts, I felt the significant weight of a woman's perspective for them. We are capable of achieving so much more together because we make up the full expression of God's image and heart.

In America, women often have not been taught how to take authority of a room full of people. Men have, though. Women have not always been encouraged to press into conflict and allow people to experience the discomfort of our confrontation as we work toward reconciliation. Most men have been doing that since the dawn of time. However, women have been allowed to identify our emotions and use them to bring resolution and care to the needy and the hurting. Women have been allowed to admit to vulnerability more openly, while men have often been discouraged from expressing themselves emotionally. The list of ways we complement one another and reflect God's image together is possibly endless, but I don't need to see it to know I want in on the battle to bring living water and the bread of life to a dying world in need of love.

The first step toward that goal is to enter the battlefield with all the ballerinas and soccer players and Baraks and Deborahs and refuse to quit until we see God's peace come to His people.

I'm in. Are you?

CHAPTER 4

THE TOO-MUCH-INFORMATION AGE

How the Information Highway Can't Save You

SOMETIMES LIFE'S GOING TO HIT YOU IN
THE HEAD WITH A BRICK. DON'T LOSE FAITH.
STEVE JOBS

I graduated from college in 1999. My kids find it preposterous that so much of my life was lived in a whole other century. But for the love of all things sane in the world, Y2K seems like it happened ten years ago to me. A complete global collapse created by the inability of all our computers to count to 2000 is still possible, right? Well, I'm hoarding bottled water and batteries just in case. I've also stocked up on gummy bears, because when society as we know it ends, I'll need a steady supply of Red No. 40 to cope until the Hunger Games are overthrown at last.

While the thirteen districts hadn't yet been formed and Katniss had yet to release her blaze of awesomeness, the keynote speaker at my 1999 UCLA College of Letters and Sciences graduation ceremony *did* mention that the rising tide of technology was changing everything about the way we lived our lives. We all nodded in agreement that day; but of course, we were actually quite naive about what lay on the horizon technologically speaking. I still owned a beeper back then. Most of us barely used our cell phones (those minutes were expensive!), and while the dot-com explosion was poised to pounce on the world, it was a very new thing and seemed to have little to do with any of us in the liberal arts community.

What's happened to us all in the past twenty years is bonkers.

If every parent today isn't lying in bed at night terrified about what their kids potentially have access to on the internet, I would like to introduce them to a little site called YouTube. There you can watch a wide variety of videos, such as dogs dancing in ballerina costumes, extended clips of NC-17 rated movies, or instructionals about how to blow stuff up using household items. If you'd like to never sleep again, dig deep into the online communities that want to teach your child how to be appropriately anorexic. The government is fighting every day to stop people from selling little girls and boys online, and yet online is where my whole family conducts research projects for science class and looks up new recipes for kombucha.[13]

Our ancestors would be very confused by this.

The internet and technology have managed to slowly take up space in our lives to completely dominate modernity. We don't know anyone's phone numbers anymore because we never have to dial them. We have no sense of direction in our own cities because GPS tells us the best way to get everywhere with the least amount of traffic, and that often means winding through random cow pastures or ancient streets that time has forgotten and we will never find again. I'm beginning to be concerned that my smartphone is actually making me dumber. My brain is never forced to remember anything because there always seems to be an app available to do the hard cognitive

---

[13] Just kidding. Kombucha is repulsive to me. I'm still getting used to Greek yogurt, for Pete's sake.

work of thinking for me.

Once upon a time, when you couldn't remember the name or the artist of the song with the line that goes "I'm never gonna dance again; guilty feet have got no rhythm," you just shrugged your shoulders and hoped it came to you eventually. You were *allowed* not to know things back then. It was frustrating not to be able to remember, of course, but also a perfectly normal part of life. After all, with only your own memory to scour for data, there were some lapses in recall you just had to accept. But now, thanks to the internet, you can type those words into your computer and—wham!—you know it was George Michael who sang those words in the song "Careless Whisper." You can even watch the video and relive MTV's heyday, or click one of the hundreds of thousands of links related to those lyrics. Sure, you had plans to mow the lawn, answer some emails, and then go to the afternoon service at church. But all that has changed now, because you ended up on Wikipedia, hopping from George Michael's page to Andrew Ridgeley's page to a page on the band Bananarama, which made you want banana bread. So you began searching for the best banana bread recipe on Pinterest, but a pin about how to train your dog not to bark caught your eye and now you're watching YouTube videos and practicing on your pup.

With all this too much information, no wonder we can't remember that we're God's set-apart people, created and called right here in the middle of our current moment as His Holy Guacamole blessing to the world. Living amid all the online and media noise is akin to trying to live in a house of mirrors. We keep looking for a reflection that makes sense, but everywhere we turn there is a distortion of our reality.

As it turns out, Walt Disney was correct: it is a small world after all. It's so tiny, in fact, it can fit in a phone the size of a fast-food napkin. But, gosh, the weight of these devices can be a heavy load to bear. In her book *The Happiness Effect: How Social Media Is Driving a Generation to Appear Perfect at Any Cost*, Donna Freitas describes our phones as portable burdens, constantly reminding us of the things we could or should be doing instead of what we are currently doing and the ways we aren't meeting other people's needs or keeping up with their lifestyles. But our relationship with these devices is one of love-hate, because, as Freitas says, they also offer us knowledge, escape, connection, and encouragement.[1]

How did we ever fit the whole world and everything we value in life into something so small? Are we capable of functioning without the internet, our handy smartphone cameras, Google Maps, text-messaging gifs, Instagram, Candy Crush, and Facebook anymore? Do we even want to try to need them less? Or have we passed the point of no return, digitally speaking?

A VACATION FROM MY PROBLEMS[14]

I accidentally stepped right in the middle of my utter dependence on my phone last year when my husband and I took a weekend getaway with a group of friends to Nashville. Our flight left before dawn, so we hauled ourselves out of bed at 4:00 a.m., filled our travel cups with coffee, and loaded the suitcases in the car. Ten minutes away from home, I realized I didn't have my phone.

"Babe, I left my phone charging on the counter."

---

[14] If you don't get this reference to the movie *What about Bob?*, please go watch it today so you can start baby-stepping through some death therapy on your way to Lake Winnipesaukee.

"We'll miss our flight if we go back."

So I became Laura Ingalls Wilder for three days.

Traveling by covered wagon and frying up corn cakes over a cow patty fire was terribly inconvenient all weekend. I kid, of course. However, walking around phoneless in an unfamiliar city did feel like becoming a pioneer in a strange new world. Apparently, I have developed a physical compulsion to check the time on my phone two hundred times every hour, so all weekend I kept asking my husband, "What time is it?" until he finally stopped answering me. When we got split up in the mall, I faced my complete inability to make a decision on my own. I needed his help choosing a pair of booties. I had no idea where he was, exactly. I couldn't text him a photo of the boots I liked to see if he thought they went with what was already in my closet. Without a phone and an internet connection, my kids had zero direct access to me, and I only spoke with them once a day (cue massive mom guilt!). I saw all sorts of lovely things I couldn't photograph and share with the masses.

In the midst of the inconvenience, I discovered there was a strange and foreign feeling of peace in this accidental technological fast. Every moment belonged to me and the actual human beings around me. I couldn't turn the conversation with the kind homeless man I met outside a restaurant one night into a tweet about perspective and joy. I couldn't Instagram a photo of me with my friend Marianne, who courageously helped me find the perfect new pair of boho/western boots when Morgan was lost to me. I savored the forgotten simplicity of living here and now, as my lightened load highlighted the value of small moments. I sat silently and watched the city pass by as we drove from the hotel to the fun places we were exploring together, marveling at how far I felt from everyone else living their fully connected lives.

In his book *The Shallows: What the Internet Is Doing to Our Brains*, Nicholas Carr offers a more scientific explanation of the weight we are all shouldering as the impact of the internet reshaping our brains and our culture.[2] As I read his analysis months later, I realized the disorientation and clarity I felt over that long weekend were those of an addict suddenly set free from her bondage of constant distraction.

I was a bird on the wing, unhindered by the weight of technology in my life. I no longer had to try to toggle back and forth between what was actually happening in front of me and everything the internet wanted to keep me informed about (for example, national news, all my friends' posts, the latest sale at The Gap). The absence of digital connection revealed how imposing the internet can be, whereas I had always thought I was merely choosing a superior way of doing my life.

I have lovely memories of that weekend. The research proves that this ought to be the case. Our constant mental juggling of information resulting from our exposure to an omnipresent media influence is causing us to forget how to remember things. To process the constant interruptions created by hyperlinks and ads, our brains, Carr writes, are becoming unable to concentrate on just one thing at a time, which means memory consolidation never happens. We skim along the surface of information so quickly we're losing the ability to create deep memories.

Given the Bible's familiar narrative about our need to remember the Lord our God, we may be in deeper trouble than we realize. The new technological age is a sort of wilderness, and we must be careful to remember who God is and who we are so we can find our way through.

Truth be told, when I arrived home after that weekend trip, I picked up my phone and went back to my scattered way of living here, there, and everywhere Google can take me. I didn't know how to be connected to the internet and yet less dependent on it. I write a blog. I pay all my bills online. My phone is my single direct connection to all my friends in the world. I did begin to fantasize about escaping the distraction of all the alerts and notifications, though. To indulge this fantasy, I have created "Airstream Days."

On Airstream Days I take a break from reality and pretend our family could live an idyllic, whimsical, internet-free life in a vintage Airstream trailer. We would cut all our ties and live on the go, camping at beaches and on mountains all over North America. The trailer would look just like one of the hundreds I have found on Pinterest: shiny silver on the outside, sleek and bohemian on the inside. Sure, six people don't even fit in an Airstream, but the one in my fantasy somehow has ample room for all of us, plus a little corner for two hundred of my favorite books.

The charm of the Airstream fantasy is that it seems possible, even though it's ridiculous. To strip our lives down to one small trailer and only the six of us to care for sounds like a dream come true. We could be one part adventurers, one part nomads, pretending that an eternal vacation has transformed all of our responsibilities and challenges into myth and lore. Laura Ingalls Wilder would approve wholeheartedly, and I could totally wear my Nashville boots. Win-win.

SHAKE THE SUGAR TREE

But while we may long to be in a vintage trailer on our way to Big Sur, God is pressing on us to remember something vital.

Like Esther, who considered the cultural threat looming over her people and chose not to hide from the chance to do something about it, we each have been born for this moment in history, with all its technological development and use.

Right here where we surf the web and search for the answers to all our obscure questions, we need to shake the sugar tree and find the water Jesus promised our friend at the well that day so long ago. She was not the first person to be thirsty for a kind of water only God could offer her. In Exodus 15, when Moses led the people of Israel through their own wilderness, at one point, they went three days without water. When they finally found water, they realized it was bitter, not sweet. They named the waters "Marah," meaning bitterness, and then they all began to freak out because the only thing worse than being thirsty and having no water is being dehydrated and having water that is not potable.

So Moses cried out to God, "and the LORD showed him a log, and he threw it into the water, and the water became sweet" (Exodus 15:25 ESV).

Imagine that. A piece of wood that sweetened water so the wandering people of God could drink and be satisfied. The Bible is full of some amazing miracles, isn't it?

The log in Exodus 15:25 is a symbol of the even greater miracle that happened on the cross. It reminds us that anytime life offers us bitter water, we can trust the Gospel to transform the bitterness into something sweet. What's more, the Hebrew verb for "show" here is the root for the word *Torah*, which means instruction or law, as in the laws God gave Moses on Mount Sinai. So God Torah-ed Moses to use the tree to make the water sweet. God's instructions and law showed Moses the way to this salvation from Israel's great need for fresh water to drink.

What can God's law do for us and our deep need to be connected? What can it do for our scattered brains, pulled in twenty different directions by the never-ending notifications and presence of the internet? We were not made to drink only the distractions and information the internet offers us. We are desperately in need of the sweet water produced by God's law and Word in our lives. If we are thirsty after trolling through Facebook, jumping to our online Bible, then clicking an article about Congress' response to the president and checking Instagram really quick, it's possible we're drinking too much of the shallow, bitter water of our culture.

God calls us to love His law and His Word more than we love all the links and clicks a search engine can offer us.

> *I have not departed from your laws, for you yourself have taught me. How sweet are your words to my taste, sweeter than honey to my mouth! I gain understanding from your precepts; therefore I hate every wrong path. (Psalm 119:102–104 NIV)*

> *Christ is the culmination of the law so that there may be righteousness for everyone who believes. (Romans 10:4 NIV)*

Therefore, we need to rest from our tendencies to seek more information in an attempt to find peace and hope. We need to heed the advice of Hebrews 4:9–13 and take a Sabbath.

REMEMBERING THE LORD OF THE SABBATH

After my weekend trip without a phone and reading *The Shallows*, I began to better grasp the sheer volume of the internet in my life. I noticed how often I was checking texts and updates and googling for information on whims. I realized how little patience I possessed as I waited for my own brain to recall what restaurants were near the baseball fields or what year a movie was released.

Somehow, I had believed the lie that if I understood and knew all life's answers, stayed connected to my many scattered friends, and kept up with everything going on in the world, I would be able to rest. But it turns out people aren't made to do that. In *The Art of Rest*, Adam Mabry writes that the pace of life in the Western world isn't physically sustainable, nor is it spiritually beneficial; however, it almost certainly guarantees that God will be slowly forgotten.[3]

Forgetting God leaves us vulnerable to all sorts of ideas, like the idea that we will have to save ourselves with our own effort and works by keeping up with the unsustainable pace our culture offers us. I was lagging in this race. I wanted to remember God, His Word, and who I was to Him and in Him.

So I began leaving my phone behind or tucking it away. I deleted Facebook and removed Safari. I loved how quiet my purse suddenly felt. In the mornings, when my phone woke me with Johnnyswim's "Paris in June," I ignored the temptation to check my email the moment my eyes opened and instead made a cup of coffee and opened God's ancient Word and asked for living water. I drew boundary lines around my life and told the internet when it was allowed to enter my holy space. My soul felt relief at last.

After all these years of living with the constant hum of the internet and the media, I needed to be reacquainted with my old friends Quiet and Stillness. My mind needed to experience a little boredom, to find its way out of the shallow waters of constant distraction. I wish it weren't so impossibly awful to sit in the waiting room at the doctor's office and refuse to check my phone, read a book, or flip through a magazine. I wish it could be easier to turn off Netflix and watch the birds from my porch and let my mind sort through all that I've heard and read and to form its own responses and thoughts accordingly. I wish there were a more "instantly downloadable" way to find peace than to sit in the quiet of my living room before everyone else wakes up, offer my prayers to God, and listen for His voice. But there isn't.

We like the internet and its distractions because they're fast and easy. God is neither of those adjectives; however, He is infinite love and endless power. If you're looking for substance and depth, He's your guy.

Chapter 4 of the book of 1 John offers a kind of guidebook for how to overcome the world's many distractions and idols. John wrote that many voices and spirits in the world will teach us that there are things that can save us apart from Jesus. The internet has offered us the false saviors of more information and online popularity and validation. But John also said Christ's love has given us the power to overcome the world's false idols. To help us know if we really grasp the love of God, John offered us a litmus test of sorts: if we love God, we will also love other people. As much as our minds want to think that our spiritual development and maturity are centered only on how we personally connect to and interact with God, the Bible always gathers us up into a corporate community of believers when we examine the quality of our faith.

We can't love other people well if we're always staring at a device. If you think that's too bold of a statement, the next time you're around someone who is on a computer or phone, assess how much love you feel in that moment. Do you feel connected when your loved one chuckles at whatever is happening on that screen? I'm not saying online interactions can't be a part of our loving relationships; but I am saying that texts and comments and messages can't replace the need we all have for the physical presence of people who love us.

IT'S TIME TO GO

I suspect the real problem the internet helps us avoid is the messiness of real-life relationships. Online discourse happens on our own terms, when it's most convenient for us. We can hide behind our screens from the call to love people as Christ has loved us: outside our own personal comfort zones. We enjoy the shallow waters of constant distraction and the entertainment of social media because it's terrifying to face the deep waters of trust, possible heartache, and our need for real love. But if we will pay attention, God is in every moment of our lives, even the terrifying ones. As an example, I offer you an average Sunday morning in my house, which could only be described as murky and slow (kind of the opposite of Google).

I've already told you how my children wake up perpetually confused on Sunday mornings about how the "going to church" thing is supposed to work. One memorable Sunday we were leaving several minutes late when someone had to run in and do "one last thing" after we were all buckled in the car and *backing out of the driveway*. I adore these sweet children of mine, but they can't be trusted to be ready to leave on time on Sunday mornings, or even Sunday afternoons. We attended the 12:30 p.m. service that day.

Worship was profound and moving, and I forgot about how I'd had to peel my progeny away from their favorite distractions to get out the door. After church, all the kids went home with friends, and Morgan and I went to lunch *alone*.[15] I left my phone in my purse on the floor of Phil's Icehouse and sat quietly at our table while Morgan got his soda. A little girl in the restaurant made eye contact with me, and I smiled at her. She came up to me and gaped through her cute pink glasses. "How old are you?" she asked. I was forced to admit that I would turn forty-two the next week, while the darling before me said she wasn't a day over six.

I wanted to tell her, "I was six once. But now I'm trapped in a middle-aged body. Total bummer," but I knew she would never believe me. Instead, I just smiled at her, and she left me to sip my tea.

Morgan and I ate chicken sandwiches, and since he was too tired to talk, he made me tell him how I was feeling about a colossal publishing disappointment that had come earlier that week. I was tasting bitter waters in the wilderness, yet simultaneously I was aware that I was in the middle of God's sovereign will.

"I feel like I'm in the back seat of a car, and I'm not completely sure if the person driving is sober."

There was a time that these feelings would have inspired an escape into Pinterest or Facebook to hide from the emotional instability that statement described. And while I wished on that day that I could know how it would all work out, I was beginning to love the feeling of letting go of my right to be in control. This strange yet comforting way faith asks us to forget ourselves and instead *be present* as we look for God's outstretched love over us was becoming more and more natural for me.

---

[15] All parents feel the same way about unexpected middle-of-the-day dates: #allwedoiswin.

Someday God is going to say something like, "It's time to go," and I hope my feet won't anchor me to the place I've been sitting all these years because I'm staring at my phone, unaware of God's presence around me. I want to rise up expectantly when He calls me, to confidently open my hand and grasp His and follow Him.

I want to remember who God is more than I want to curate a decent online following or have kids who are on time or achieve a wicked excellent career. There is a powerful old song, penned by hymnwriter Isaac Watts, that Siri and Alexa would never think to suggest as a way to draw us into the God of All Things, and yet it does:

> *Come, Holy Spirit, heavenly Dove,*
> *with all thy quickening powers;*
> *kindle a flame of sacred love*
> *in these cold hearts of ours.*
>
> *See how we trifle here below,*
> *fond of these earthly toys:*
> *our souls, how heavily they go,*
> *to reach eternal joys.*
>
> *In vain we tune our formal songs,*
> *in vain we strive to rise:*
> *hosannas languish on our tongues,*
> *and our devotion dies.*
>
> *Come, Holy Spirit, heavenly Dove,*
> *with all thy quickening powers;*
> *come, shed abroad a Savior's love,*
> *and that shall kindle ours.*

This song is a good reminder that while the internet and all its information are new places to learn the discipline of trusting God, our need for the power of the Holy Spirit is not new. Faith is an ancient pathway requiring the mysterious, transformative fire of the Holy Spirit to raise us out of our slow ways and remind us to remember the Lord our God and His greatest commandment.

Jesus didn't tell us to find out the answer to every question we could ever ask. He didn't instruct us to run away from the world when the burdens of our lives became too complicated. Jesus said to love God with your heart, soul, and mind, and your neighbor as yourself (Mark 12:30–31). He also said: "In this world you will have trouble. But take heart! I have overcome the world" (John 16:33 NIV).

As we navigate our lives, so rich with complex relationships and circumstances, it's probably going to seem like the driver of our car is a little dizzy or distracted. More information or online connection will not give us more control or insure us against possible calamity or injury. Remembering that Jesus has asked us to recognize the troubles we face and to set our hearts on His promise to rescue us will offer us a safe place to wait for His redemption, confident simply in *being* the Holy Guacamole He made us to be.

If you have to put your phone down for an afternoon or two and sit in the silence, waiting for God's peace to surpass your understanding, crack open your Y2K water bottles and just do it.

It'll be worth the sacrifice. I promise.

CHAPTER 5

THE PERFECT STORM
How Perfectionism Can't Save You

I recently attended a wedding in which the bride and groom recited their own vows. I always love when people do this, partly because I'm a word person and I like to hear the words people choose to proclaim their love and partly because people are just funny about what they choose to say. At this particular wedding, the groom promised the bride he would "never do anything to hurt you, ever."

I fell over dead on the spot.

While I appreciate this groom's earnestness and devotion, I would bet you a million lattes that vow was broken before the honeymoon ended. No man is perfect enough to never do anything to hurt his wife. He could wake up one morning with too much stubble, and she could take it personally all day. In fact, it hurts my feelings to even *imagine* my husband promising me that he will never hurt my feelings.[16]

---

[16] Just go ahead and apologize now, Morgan. Even though you did nothing and I created this whole problem by writing this chapter. I forgive you for what you never said or did. I still love you. The end.

But I get the spirit of that groom's promise of perfection. Love is supposed to be perfect. Every detail of a wedding is supposed to be perfect—and there are a lot of details to weddings these days. That poor guy just wanted to join in the fun and promise to love his new wife perfectly. It's sweet.

I feel fortunate to be what you could call a PPB: pre-Pinterest bride. For all of you who were born after 1990 or who got married after Pinterest and its bounty of detailed DIY inspiration debuted, I'm here to testify those creative wedding ideas used to require much more effort. We had only our friends and *Martha Stewart Weddings* magazines to rely on. We couldn't google "boho wedding photo ideas" to show examples of what we wanted to a photographer or florist, because as shocking as this may be, Google didn't exist then. Email was the only real use we had for the internet.

In this prehistoric era, unless you had the big bucks to hire a professional wedding planner, the whole affair was pretty simple to arrange: choose the dresses, flowers, menu, and venue. There was less pressure to execute all the tiny details perfectly. We didn't have to source chalk-painted antique doors for our guests to pass through or smoke bombs to set off in our photographs. The downside to this low pressure for me, a not-so-detail-oriented person, was that I didn't know what I was doing, and I felt no particular pressure to figure it out. If you're wondering if that means my wedding was a slipshod mess of potential disasters, you would be correct. To loosely summarize and riff off the Fresh Prince: this is a story all about how my wedding plans got flipped-turned upside down.

MY KINKO'S INVITATIONS: #GETJEALOUS

My slacker problems began with the invitations. In 2001, brides-to-be were still fairly traditional and bound by rules of etiquette created by women wearing white gloves and hats. I couldn't afford hand-calligraphed linen parchment, so I went to Kinko's,[17] ordered white invitations with fancy writing on them, and called it a day. Once we addressed them by hand and bought some stamps, we sent them to everyone our parents told us to send them to, because we were good children.[18]

One perfect detail we had down was the proper stamp selection. When I think back on those LOVE stamps I bought for our invitations, I get all kinds of warm, fuzzy feelings about all I achieved by refusing to buy basic American flag stamps. Compared to the cost of stamps now, my pretty wedding stamps cost tuppence a piece. Why is mail so expensive in the twenty-first century? Do we use actual trained homing pigeons to deliver all these letters? I don't understand how I can't afford to send out a hundred Christmas cards, but the Chinese restaurant around the corner can afford to mail me three hundred menus every year.[19] But I digress. Back to the imperfect wedding saga.

Once we sent our invitations, a friend came to me and pointed out that I had not included a map to the wedding location. This was not only the ancient pre-Pinterest days; it was also the pre–Google Maps days, and most people expected to be given some kind of map or directions to the wedding venue. I guess I was supposed to either draw a map myself

---

[17] Can you even believe I ordered wedding invitations from Kinko's? If you are too young to know what Kinko's was, imagine a UPS store that won't mail anything for you. I know. It makes no sense.

[18] My parents are my heroes. They actually offered us the cash they had saved for my wedding if we didn't want to have a big shindig. I was tempted to take the money and go to Vegas, but Morgan said we needed a day of celebration. He's so cute and secretly romantic. But I think he regretted that decision a few months later when we sat and cried together on our only piece of furniture because we had $17.83 in the bank. #youliveandlearn #broke

[19] Please email me if you can resolve my mail ponderings or recommend an excellent nonauthentic, super-Americanized Chinese restaurant in the Austin area, because I don't like the real stuff.

or call the venue and ask them to mail me a copy of a map, then make copies of the map and stuff them in every invitation before sending them out.[20]

But that was too hard for me to execute, so I eschewed all responsibility for a map. This is how the conversation with my helpful friend went:

> Friend: "Some people have complained that you didn't include a map."
> Me: "I know. It was too hard. I couldn't figure it out."
> Friend: "They can't come if they don't know where it is."
> Me: "Can't they look it up—you know. . .on their own map? I mean, it's at a botanical garden at a major university."
> Friend: "People won't do that. They just won't come."
> Me: "I will miss seeing them."[21]

My friend was correct. Some people didn't come because I didn't include maps with the invitations. Those poor people missed a seriously righteous dance party after the "I do's" were done that day. Morgan and I probably missed out on a few more place settings of our formal china because they didn't come. But since we never used the china we did receive, I'm not that sad about it. At the time I hardly noticed who was coming or not coming, though, because of the weather forecast.

---

[20] Kinko's probably could have helped with that too. But I didn't want to go back there. It was such a sad place that smelled like ink and bad design.

[21] *Speak to the hand. Deuces, haters. Bye, Felicia.*

IT NEVER RAINS IN SOUTHERN CALIFORNIA

It actually *does* rain in Southern California every now and then. In fact, in 2001 the weather forecast predicted a massive storm the whole weekend of our mid-March outdoor wedding. We had no backup plan. We had only our prayers and my parents' living room, which could seat about eight people. The night before the wedding, it rained so hard the caterer for our rehearsal dinner was two hours late. Even Pinterest couldn't have helped us avoid this near-catastrophic situation.

But by then, I didn't care any longer about perfect anything. All I cared about was getting married to Morgan. I would have married him in the rain. I would have married him on a train. I would've married Morgan here or there. I'd have married him anywhere.

Thankfully, I didn't have to marry Morgan in the rain or on a train.[22] We woke up to a miraculous clear California spring day on March 10, 2001.

I was determined that nothing else would go wrong. My positive attitude delivered.

The wedding coordinator fell flat on her face after she straightened my train as I walked down the aisle. I found this adorably cute. As we took our vows, a giant spider lowered itself onto my bare shoulder from the palm tree over our heads. I laughed and blew it off, literally. We forgot to eat a piece of our wedding cake before it was all gone, but I hardly noticed because all that mattered was that Morgan and I were in love, happy, and married.

If we set our eyes on the love we share, perfectionism loses the battle for our attention. Living a Holy Guacamole

---

[22] There should be more weddings in the rain on trains. That actually sounds incredibly romantic.

life allows us to enjoy the day and let God's perfect sacrifice do its thing. Perfection, schmerfection.

Pinterest didn't invent the pressure to be perfect. Even the most casual glance into history reveals humanity's common quest for a way to save ourselves by perfect obedience and performance. Jesus Himself warned the people of His day not to succumb to the tantalizing path of outward perfection.

> *"Woe to you, scribes and Pharisees, hypocrites! For you clean the outside of the cup and the plate, but inside they are full of greed and self-indulgence. You blind Pharisee! First clean the inside of the cup and the plate, that the outside also may be clean." (Matthew 23:25–26 ESV)*

There has probably never been an era that didn't value and reward outward perfection of some kind. Without a little grace and redemption, most of us try to be like the Pharisees and get our acts together on the outside, because we all know what's inside is much more complicated to get right. Printing a perfect map is easy. Blazing a new trail while blinded by our deep human need is not.

The first time I remember hearing our cultural message about perfection being the ultimate goal in life was when I was seven and saw the original movie *The Stepford Wives*. It seems strange to me now that at such a young age, I was allowed to watch a film about murderous husbands replacing their imperfect wives with perfect robot copies. But it was on prime-time television, so it was edited and likely considered harmless. It's possible we had a babysitter that night and she assumed the movie's complex story line would be over my head.

Given that I only remember two scenes from the movie

(a robot woman malfunctioning over tea and the chase scene at the end), I suppose it *was* over my head. But I assure you, I understood the plot. I even formed a lovely fear that *it was real.* Like many small children, I thought everything on television was real.

For a few years after the *Stepford Wives*–watching event, I wondered if I was the only real human around. I watched everyone for signs of robotness. I tried to imagine what kinds of mechanical wonders existed under their false human facades. I worried that they all knew I was the only real, imperfect person left.

It's possible this fear was the first step onto a path marked for future therapy. It's also possible that it was merely one stop along a road that would lead me to the truth that I would never measure up to perfection.

It seems like horrible news to hear, doesn't it?

However, all along my winding path, through childhood and into my adult life, God has had plans that were better for me than my ability to save myself. The horrible news that I would never be perfect meant I was off the hook. God was inviting the same girl who sent out map-less wedding invitations to throw out her perfect china and dance on the broken pieces. A Holy Guacamole life means trusting that God's own perfect plan is always leading us to the best party ever, whether or not we know the way through ourselves.

All we need to get there is a super-holy lamb.

A PERFECT LAMB

The peculiar and mystical thing about our God is that He actually *does* require perfect holiness and obedience from His children, and yet He lovingly admits we are wholly incapable of achieving it on our own. This strange dichotomy is the reason Jesus offered Himself as our substitute, so that we could receive His perfect, blameless record: "For by one sacrifice he has made perfect forever those who are being made holy" (Hebrews 10:14 NIV).

Given the lack of perfection we see in the people of Jesus, the word "perfect" here can't mean being the most beautiful, talented, intelligent, admired, and esteemed people possible. It can't mean free from error, because the text says we are "being made holy." Perfection is clearly different from holiness. The Greek word for "perfect" in this passage is *teleioō*, and it means to be made complete or fulfilled. The Greek word here for "holy" is *hagiazō*, which means to be purified, to be made free from sin, and to be internally renewed in your soul.

So Hebrews 10:14 is telling us that Jesus fulfilled and completed us, and now we can enjoy the life He offers us, becoming purer and freer as we go.

Given that this process of purification seems to be God's map to our final destination, maybe we put too much pressure on ourselves to appear flawless and to perform perfectly along the way.

In our hearts we know perfectionism won't save us, and yet the flesh attempts it anyway. Most of us just cross our fingers that when the wind blows our proverbial skirts a little too high, we're wearing acceptable underwear.

But even if we have on a pair of sensible shorts under everything, life can be full of humiliation if the people around us aren't too keen on grace. Even in the churchy world of Christianity.

EVEN THE FIRST LADIES

The irony that I ended up a pastor's wife, which is about as close to Stepford wife territory as a girl can get, is not lost on me. I don't know what toxic mixture of pride and prejudice has cultivated this church culture in America where the pastor's wife (and pretty much everyone else) feels pressure to be perceived as perfect.

Maybe this book is my grand chance to malfunction and show the world that I am just like everyone else. We all share a common predicament, namely, our need to be loved in the midst of our imperfections. Can we end the madness and agree to stop trying to look like we don't need the mercy, grace, and forgiveness Jesus offered us on the cross? Because really, what's the point of pursuing perfection if God already knows otherwise about us and told us He would take care of it?

> *"Then what if you were to see the Son of Man ascending to where he was before? It is the Spirit who gives life; the flesh is no help at all. The words that I have spoken to you are spirit and life. But there are some of you who do not believe." (For Jesus knew from the beginning who those were who did not believe, and who it was who would betray him.) And he said, "This is why I told you that no one can come to me unless it is granted him by the Father." (John 6:62–65 ESV)*

The flesh is no help at all, Jesus said. Our human ability renders us useless as saviors in the grand scheme of spiritual matters. Perfect performance won't raise us above our spiritual deadness. Perfect obedience can't save us. Nothing we do can make us good enough to avoid our need to eat and drink the death, burial, and resurrection of Christ.

Years ago, Morgan and I faced some news that several leaders we knew personally had committed deeply immoral acts involving abuses of power, greed, and infidelity. I thought of the hundreds of times I had heard these people testify to how God had rescued them from sin and brokenness years before. I thought of all that following Jesus had cost them once upon a time. I knew they loved God deeply, and I mourned all they had lost because of their poor choices and sinful acts.

Something was missing in their stories, though. We had followed them for years and had never heard them speak of their own weaknesses. For reasons I can't explain, these leaders had felt the need to look perfect and sinless to the world. I realized then that no one is more insecure than the person who must hide all traces of vulnerability. They either have never been taught or have forgotten that their imperfections and weaknesses are the places where God's love and strength become glorious testimonies of grace and mercy to a world terrified it will never measure up or be enough.

To admit our own shady imperfection, we need the humble story of a God-King who was born in a manger to an unwed woman. There isn't much perfect about how Christ entered the world. And yet His birth was miraculous and beautiful.

Where can we go to remember that miracles aren't perfect photos we can pin up to prove we're worthy of love? I want to say we can go to church, but I realize that statement might be met with some eye-rolling. Many churches have not historically been places of brave imperfection and vulnerability.

But that doesn't mean they shouldn't be.

IMPERFECT CHURCHES

A healthy church is a place of refuge from Pinterest perfection, Facebook rants, and glossy Instagram posts. It's a place you can show up with all of who you are, even the parts that seem a little messy or (gasp!) not so biblically sound. It's a safe place to bring your questions and fears and insecurities and pride. A healthy church is a family full of people who value humility, repentance, growth, forgiveness, and honor for others.

As long as we are hustling to prove we're perfect enough to deserve respect, validation, or approval, we are unable to offer those same gifts to others who are also less than perfect. If my only goal is cultivating a perfect me, I lose my place in the greater story of God's will. And yet if I completely ignore my own personal development, I risk becoming a liability in my community at large.

How do we grow in Christlikeness while remaining in unity with the people around us? If our own perfection can't save us, what's our goal supposed to be? Surely we aren't supposed to show up with our imperfections waving like flags above us, are we?

To answer those questions, I offer you the story of my first women's event at our church after we became pastors. (I have so many regrets, you guys.)

For our inaugural women's event, we decided to have a mother-daughter tea. We sewed pretty table runners and borrowed tea sets from twenty people. We made lemon curd and scones. I showed up early and rolled tables into the meeting room. A facilities volunteer saw me shoving those tables through the sanctuary and shook his head. "What kind of pastor's wife does that?"

I could have answered with, "The kind who wants everything to be perfect and would rather not ask for help," but I was too busy busting it for my Jane Austen–style dream.

Once the women arrived, we ate tiny cakes and sipped hot tea while several visiting ministers spoke on generational legacy. They were fantastic. We were winning in a million ways. When they finished, I closed the gathering with a quick prayer and excused everyone.

Except "everyone" wasn't pleased with me or my perfect leadership of the morning.

A woman I recognized but didn't know approached me, fuming about the way I ended the gathering. Her rebuke was fully thought out and hit its mark. She accused me of ruining the moment for God and for many of the women. She told me I had mishandled the Holy Spirit by failing to ask the women ministering to end it the way she believed it should have ended.

I was stunned and out of my depth. My heart pounded. I fumbled my way through our conversation. After she walked away, I went into the bathroom and cried in a stall by myself. Either this woman had misunderstood my honest attempt at serving our women as fear and incompetence, or she was correct and I was afraid and incompetent. Either way, I was far from perfect.

What do we do when we fail to be perfect? How do we chew the meat of criticism that can help us to grow and yet spit out the bones of our misunderstandings that threaten to choke the life out of us? How can we grow in love despite our imperfections?

Eventually, to grow in love for God and for others, we must step away from our individualistic ideas about perfection and toward relationships and community.

A FAR BETTER WAY

First Corinthians 13 offers a wonderful biblical definition of love. How many weddings have we attended where we were reminded by Paul's ancient letter to Corinth of how love is patient and kind; it believes the best and bears all things; love never fails and it never ends? The passage is positively swoon worthy.

While it's true a marriage built with that kind of love as the cement has a shot at lasting a lifetime, 1 Corinthians 13 wasn't originally written as an attempt to describe the kind of love we should have for our spouses. It's not even about marriage. The chapter describes what the church should be. We can see that clearly when we flip back and read the words that set up this famous passage:

> *You are Christ's body—that's who you are! You must never forget this. Only as you accept your part of that body does your "part" mean anything. You're familiar with some of the parts that God has formed in his church, which is his "body.". . .*
>
> *But it's obvious by now, isn't it, that Christ's church is a complete Body and not a gigantic, unidimensional Part? It's not all Apostle, not all Prophet, not all Miracle Worker, not all Healer, not all Prayer in Tongues, not all Interpreter of Tongues. And yet some of you keep competing for so-called "important" parts.*
>
> *But now I want to lay out a far better way for you.*
>
> *If I speak with human eloquence and angelic ecstasy but don't love, I'm nothing but the creaking of a rusty gate.*
>
> *If I speak God's Word with power, revealing all his*

*mysteries and making everything plain as day, and if I
have faith that says to a mountain, "Jump," and it jumps,
but I don't love, I'm nothing.*

*If I give everything I own to the poor and even go to
the stake to be burned as a martyr, but I don't love, I've
gotten nowhere. (1 Corinthians 12:27–13:3 MSG)*

First Corinthians 12 and 13 are meant to inspire us to create communities that validate and celebrate how different we all are as we love one another. Paul was saying that no matter how supreme our giftings and talents may be, our ability to love as he defined it—to be patient, kind, not boastful, not self-seeking, always forgiving, etc.— is irreplaceable. Church isn't supposed to be full of people who are all perfect carbon copies of each other. The reason love is so essential to the Body of Christ is because people are going to be imperfect and fail and then *need that kind of love.*

Yet I've been in churches where I was shamed for my imperfections. We've seen how church leaders can abuse power in damaging ways. I meet people all the time who no longer attend any church because they were wounded by the people there who were supposed to love them. It's heartbreaking to know the Body of Christ has failed God and people to the degree it has.

But I hope we will all keep believing for redemption and keep working toward a better story. Sometimes you just have to get back on the horse that threw you. I mean that figuratively about church, but I also mean it literally about horses.

When I was growing up, we spent many of our summers visiting my great-grandparents in Frederick, Oklahoma. They were cattle ranchers and cotton farmers, and for a week or two of every year I traded my totally rad California beach days for the red dirt country life. My favorite part was the horses.

One year, I rode a horse named Schoolboy out along the edge of their property alone. Schoolboy had once been a champion barrel racer, but by the time I rode him, he was a fairly old, docile horse. The ride away from the house was perfectly tranquil and lovely.

When we made the turn back, though, old Schoolboy got a little excited. I had relaxed and given him lots of rein. Fast horses love lots of rein. Old horses love going home. As a young rider, I got scared when he shot off toward the main road by the house. In an attempt to stay in the saddle, my knees tightened, which sent a clear message to Schoolboy: *Run faster!*

We were barreling along the fence line toward the road at breakneck speed. When Schoolboy got to the road, he made a sharp right turn around the fence post that I did not anticipate. Schoolboy went right, but I kept going forward. I flew off that horse and landed on the ground.

Whose fault was it? Mine, in part, for giving the horse so much rein and not knowing my horse well enough. But it was also his. Schoolboy was well trained and aware he was out for a walk, perhaps a trot. He knew this was no rodeo. Neither one of us performed our roles perfectly that day. I got hurt when I fell, and my uncle Wayne made sure Schoolboy knew he had behaved very badly.

Later, Wayne and my dad made me get back on the horse—for the good of both of us. I needed to ride again to conquer my fear. Schoolboy needed me to ride him again so he could prove he had learned his lesson. I held the reins shorter and sat more relaxed in the saddle this time when we turned back for home.

Our goal as the Church is to offer an imperfect world the grace and truth of God. We haven't always carried everyone safely home. We have run too fast, taken corners too sharply. Some of us have not followed the instructions Jesus gave us, and we have been poor leaders or poor followers. Sin and errors have been left unchecked and unrepented. Some of us have ended up on the ground, worse for wear. Some of us have lost the people we were carrying, because we got excited or misunderstood the signals and messages they were sending us. Many of us walk alone now as a result of these misunderstandings. The thought of this lonely road is a heartache I can hardly bear.

And yet we are all headed home, one way or another. The goal is to learn from our mistakes, repent, forgive, and get back on that horse to try again.

I don't know exactly what turn your current path is taking today, but I know that God is leading us all into an eternal community. God longs for us to experience the joy and delight our triune God experiences every day in His own perfect community of love: Father, Son, and Spirit.

Someday there will be a kind of wedding to end all weddings. Revelation 19 tells us that when that perfect day comes, we will hear a loud multitude crying out, "Hallelujah!" (v. 6). Every time we reach out past our imperfection to love and serve others, we are making the Bride of Christ more perfect, readier for Jesus to return for her. When He returns, He will heal all the pain left from the ways others didn't love us well. He will perfect every imperfection, and we will enter into a kind of forever love we can only imagine here on earth.

We will be blessed to be invited to that wedding, and we won't need a map or a cloudless day to get there. The final turn home won't throw us to the ground, but we will want to bow low before Him and worship Him. We can begin to bring His kingdom to earth by living on our knees here, loving all the imperfect people around us the way God has loved us—like a groom and bride who promise to always be in it together, no matter what.

CHAPTER 6

PLEASE EXCUSE THE WOOD PALLET WALL IN MY EYE

How Cynicism Can't Save You

TO HAVE COURAGE FOR WHATEVER COMES
IN LIFE—EVERYTHING LIES IN THAT.
ST. TERESA OF AVILA

Does your church have a wood pallet wall?

The wood pallet craze has died down a little in the past few years, but for a while there, what was hotter than free wood ripped apart and then hammered onto sheetrock? We were all crazy for this trend. Our church has at least three rooms with wood pallet walls. They make a beautiful backdrop for family photos and were an inexpensive way to add character to our otherwise very dated 1970s building. Our wood walls were all a labor of love by people we love, and so they are meaningful to us and feel more like part of our story than just a design choice.

I wonder, though, what will happen to those walls when the design trends change and wood pallet walls fall out of fashion. Will we simply move on to the next trend, or will we find a way to honor what we love about these walls by incorporating them into the story of our church in new ways? If the day ever comes that wood pallet walls are offensive to people, what on earth will we do about that?

But surely I'm being ridiculous. It can't be possible for a church to have the "wrong kind of walls," can it? Am I over-thinking wood walls?

Possibly. However, given the general cynicism in the world about churches, I admit I tend to overthink almost everything church related.

Do I need to explain how cynical we have become as a society? Should we go into a deep analysis of all the ways immoral leadership and abuses of power have caused people who love God to look sideways at organized religion? Should we dissect how hard it is when people we love take advantage of us in the name of their faith?

Or can we all just agree that we're a little worn out from the push and pull of some church experiences?

The result of our general cultural cynicism about corrupt power structures is that church members struggle to find a church they feel safe in and, likewise, pastors and leaders struggle to build an environment where everyone feels safe, since we often don't all agree on what a safe space actually looks like.

When our capitalistic society intersects this cynicism, we find the Western church world is ripe with people who don't feel safe or happy in our churches and who will leave if they think they can find something better somewhere else. They often can. Which leads to a strange and interesting fact: sometimes the people who feel most cynical about the way the Church is failing are the people leading it, because they feel like they can never do enough or be enough to meet everyone's expectations, and eventually, everyone will leave them to go somewhere else.

Personally, my husband and I have lived this tale of woe,

and we have watched Jesus turn cynicism into hope like He once made water into wine.

Before we became the lead pastors, lots of people had been leaving our church. It was in a death spiral: not much money, a reduced number of staff members, and everyone had dear friends leaving. After we were hired as the pastors, many, many, many, many, many more people left.[23] Transitions are hard on weary and wounded communities. Not everyone wanted to stay to see if the church would survive.

On our first Sunday, a woman came up to Morgan after the sermon and asked him to pray for her.

"Pastor, I need you to pray for me. I'm trying to figure out if I should leave this church or not now that you're here," she said.

If you don't think God has a good sense of humor, then you haven't spent enough time with Him. He can turn the most rejecting moments of today into the best jokes of your future. Many more people left after this woman's vulnerable and fairly offensive prayer request. At one point, our church that had bought a building when it had about 800 people attending had barely 150 walking through the doors on any given Sunday.

Every email and conversation that began with, "We feel like God is calling us somewhere else. . ." felt like failure. I thought most of the pain came from the reality that every departure back then meant the church might not make it at all. I thought the weight we felt was because empty chairs are depressing, and empty offices meant there wasn't enough staff to

---

[23] Did you notice all the times I wrote the word *many*? I was trying to capture the sheer volume of people who left because we had become the pastors. The publisher made me edit this sentence. In the original manuscript, the word *many* repeated here one billion times. As you can imagine, this experience was a huge boost to our confidence.

shoulder the work. I thought that if we could save the church, get money in the bank, and fill the seats with people, then we wouldn't feel so broken when someone left.

I was wrong. People Who Leave will always feel like a broken heart.

Many years later, once the church had grown and was healthy and stable, some of our closest friends left our church. Their departure devastated us. In Matthew 18:12–13 Jesus said:

> *"What do you think? If a man has a hundred sheep, and one of them has gone astray, does he not leave the ninety-nine on the mountains and go in search of the one that went astray? And if he finds it, truly, I say to you, he rejoices over it more than over the ninety-nine that never went astray." (ESV)*

I always wonder if Jesus was thinking about Judas when He told that story. I'm fairly certain He was thinking about me and all the times cynicism would threaten to cut me off from His redemptive plans in the midst of my pain.

I know I'm not supposed to write about People Who Leave Your Church. In the world of Christianity, the word *taboo* does not begin to adequately define this particular topic. The shame associated with people leaving a church is so great that pastors don't talk a lot about this, except in quiet counseling offices with downcast eyes and hushed voices. No one wants to hear how painful it is to feel like you've failed people you were called to shepherd.

But everyone needs to know that in any moment of betrayal or loss, it is Jesus alone who meets us and reminds us that even when His best friends deserted Him, it was not the end of God's plan for redemption.

NON-CHURCHY BETRAYALS

Perhaps people have never left your church, so you're wondering what the big deal is. I would wager that if we dug around a little in your life, we would find a place where someone or some entity disappointed you. Betrayal cut into your soul a bit when you felt deserted in either a literal or a figurative sense. I would also predict that your heart was at least tempted to harden as a result and become cynical about the way trusting people or systems of power is a potential mistake.

A politician who was elected to serve you may have said something that caused you to feel marginalized or angry. A parent may have broken promises to you, enforcing the message that you needed to take care of yourself. A friend who was supposed to know better may have taken something from you, like your ability to rely on others.

Or perhaps you have been slowly worn down by all the bad news. Governmental overthrows, starving people, sex trafficking, rampant disease, children working in factories for pennies a day, poverty that can't be overcome, the marginalization of whole people groups. It doesn't take long to find reasons to be cynical about the failure of systems of authority in the world, even when our personal lives are doing just fine.

So much fear is involved when betrayal strikes our hearts. We fear that others will follow suit (some usually do). We sometimes fear that we are partly to blame, and that if we had been stronger/better/wiser we wouldn't be in so much pain. We fear that we are more alone than we realize.

So we grab some scrap wood called cynicism and use it

to cover up the bare walls of our souls. The bad news is that a wood wall isn't enough to cover our true vulnerability to evil. The good news is that even when we feel deserted, left alone on life's plate like those rice and beans I told you about, God is here at the table declaring we're still the Holiest Guacamole he ever made, and He's never going to leave us alone.

In his book *The Wounded Healer*, Henri Nouwen described the plight of modernity way back in the 1970s, pointing out the paradoxical weight of all we can accomplish through technology and our powerlessness to end things like poverty and oppression.[1] If the past fifty years since Nouwen wrote that book have proven anything, it is that living in the dualism of our great human potential and our enormous human frailty has weakened our resistance to cynicism. We don't trust the media, the government, schools, or the Church. But when we levy our complaints, we conveniently forget that we are each actually *members* of all those entities, and so our pointing fingers eventually point back at ourselves.

Jesus pointed all this out in Matthew 7. He didn't talk about wood walls, but He did talk about logs and specks in our eyes:

> *"Judge not, that you be not judged. For with the judgment you pronounce you will be judged, and with the measure you use it will be measured to you. Why do you see the speck that is in your brother's eye, but do not notice the log that is in your own eye? Or how can you say to your brother, "Let me take the speck out of your eye," when there is the log in your own eye? You hypocrite, first take the log out of your own eye, and then you will see clearly to take the speck out of your brother's eye." (vv. 1–5 ESV)*

This is how I imagine any conversation with Jesus regarding all the injustices in the world might go:

> Jesus: "*Do you see a problem in the world, in your church, in your government, or in the life of someone you know?*"
>
> Us: "Yes. We see lots of problems in all of those places."
>
> Jesus: "*Good. Don't become cynical. Make sure you aren't creating part of the problem, then go help sort it out.*"

Of course, it's rarely that simple.

Have you ever had something stuck in your eye? It's horrific. A few years ago, I had something really, really stuck in my eye. I kept rinsing it and closing it and crying and rinsing it some more, and the thing wouldn't come out. I lay down on the bed and made my slightly squeamish husband use a flashlight and root around under my eyelid to try to find the speck. He shook his head and told me it looked fine. I believe his exact words were: "Nope! Shipshape! Maybe you *had* something in there, but you rinsed it out and it left a scratch on your eye."[24]

I nodded and held my eye shut all night, but I knew Captain Positive Thinking was wrong. I could feel the speck in my eye. But it didn't feel like a speck; it felt like a boulder or possibly Sputnik was lodged beneath my eyelid. I was incapable of doing anything so long as it was there. I couldn't take care of my kids. I couldn't read. I couldn't even listen to anyone speak because I was in constant agony. No one seemed to understand

---

[24] In the immortal words of the great prophet C-3PO, "We seem to be made to suffer. It's our lot in life."

the pain I was in. I felt alone and useless and like my whole world had been swallowed up by the pain in my eye.

So I went to the eye doctor.

My eye doctor used her weird eye microscope and some dye to go on an eye-speck expedition. Lo and behold, she found a microbead from my face cleanser lodged in my eyeball, and she had to use a needle to remove it.[25] Vanity is a curse, isn't it?

Ever since then I've thought about how a tiny, insignificant problem like a microbead in my eye could consume me. Likewise, Jesus warned us about specks in our eyes knowing that one tiny sin or wound is capable of incapacitating us for the work He has called us to do. Our efforts to ignore our problems will only cause greater pain and disconnection.

If some sin, injustice, disloyalty, or betrayal has gotten in our spiritual eyes, we must follow Jesus' teaching and apply God's judgment to ourselves first. Cynicism is an attempt to shield ourselves from God's judgment. It's a special kind of self-deception that says forgiveness and mercy are lost hopes, so why not just give up on anything ever getting better?

When Peter wrote to the churches in Asia Minor, I think he was hoping his instructions would help them avoid any wood walls or eye specks among them:

> *Be self-controlled and sober-minded for the sake of your prayers. Above all, keep loving one another earnestly, since love covers a multitude of sins. Show hospitality to one another without grumbling. As each has received a*

---

[25] I felt like I was in a Tom Cruise sci-fi movie and my visual memories were about to be harvested as I watched that needle hover over my retina. Thankfully, my eye doctor is a regular person and not an evil genius who is trying to take over the world.

gift, use it to serve one another, as good stewards of God's varied grace: whoever speaks, as one who speaks oracles of God; whoever serves, as one who serves by the strength that God supplies—in order that in everything God may be glorified through Jesus Christ. To him belong glory and dominion forever and ever. (1 Peter 4:7–11 ESV)

Maybe Peter was right, and a little hospitality is in order. I wonder what kind of glory would appear if we tore down our wood walls and built one long table so we could sit down to a meal of grace-infused fajitas, chips, and Holy Guacamole together.

A TABLE CALLED HOPE

A few Christmases ago, a friend of ours invited his father, who was a committed agnostic, to church on Christmas Eve. That particular Christmas season fell in the middle of a very painful election here in America. Negativity, fake news, and lots of fighting in the media swirled around us. Polarization ripped through our country as we decorated trees and baked Christmas cookies.

Our friend's father walked through the parking lot of the church, past bumper stickers promoting opposing candidates, and into a sanctuary full of homeless people, those belonging to the middle class, and folks with ample wealth. These people spanned diverse races and ethnicities. He held a candle and passed a flame to the stranger next to him as everyone sang "Silent Night." When the service was over, he turned to his son and said, "I don't know about all the Jesus stuff, but this place gives me hope."

Isn't that what the Church is supposed to do—offer a

broken, cynical, doubting world a little hope that, possibly, there is a kind of belonging that can save us from the painful ways we've been separated?

I know church is messy. Good grief, life and people are messy. We arrive everywhere with our mess, which is why it's hard to live in peace as a community. There were probably people at that same Christmas Eve service who had concerns about the music, the way the pastor preached, or the way some part of the service might have made someone else feel. For all we know, those people carried their criticisms out the door, without telling anyone, to another church they hoped would do things differently. It's a shame, really, because we all lose the chance to grow when this happens. Universal peace and harmony are impossible to find everywhere—in our homes, in our workplaces, in traffic jams, in our social media feeds, in our schools, in our governments, and in our churches. But that doesn't mean we should stop believing for the miracle or leave the table forever.

Any brief study of the epistles proves that Jesus' followers are called to seek justice and freedom while remaining connected to each other. Paul offered practical ways to relate to other believers amid all the mess:

Rejoice with those who rejoice, weep with those who weep. Live in harmony with one another. Do not be haughty, but associate with the lowly. Never be wise in your own sight. Repay no one evil for evil, but give thought to do what is honorable in the sight of all. If possible, so far as it depends on you, live peaceably with all. Beloved, never avenge yourselves, but leave it to the wrath of God, for it is written, "Vengeance is mine, I will

repay, says the Lord." To the contrary, "if your enemy is
hungry, feed him; if he is thirsty, give him something
to drink; for by so doing you will heap burning coals on
his head." Do not be overcome by evil, but overcome
evil with good. (Romans 12:15–21 ESV)

Our problem of church messiness is not new, and neither is God's solution. God has given us a seat at the table with the hope that we will grab a sponge and clean some of the mess ourselves.

But who am I to speak of cleaning messes? I don't even clean my own house.

In fact, every other week, two precious women come and clean my house for me. I pay them, of course. It's an indulgence, to pay to have my house cleaned. It hasn't always been like this.[26] However, after three babies entered our family in a span of twenty-seven months, I became a walking zombie who no longer cared about anything except keeping her children alive. Morgan grew weary of living in filth and insisted we hire someone to clean for us.

Mercy set me free, and I never looked back.

The irony of having a cleaning crew bust a move in your house, though, is that you have to preclean for them. This is particularly true for my family, which accommodates three teenagers, one very cute preteen, and eight bazillion after-school activities. We live like frat boys in college for the two weeks between holy visits of the cleaning ladies. The night

---

[26] Before I had babies, I used to scrub my floors on my hands and knees every week. I cleaned the baseboards every week. I dusted every surface, removed everything from the kitchen counters and scoured them with disinfectant. I even cleaned the kitchen and bathroom cabinets and all the windows in the house every. single. week. I mourn all the days I could have just sprawled myself on the sofa reading a book while eating donuts back then. I was so blind to my privilege.

before they come, we pick up the junk we've piled on the stairs and the dining room table. We tuck away the toothpaste caps rolling around on the countertop and gather up three loads of dirty laundry from the boys' bathroom floor. We sort through the wretched little heaps of mail in the kitchen.

Then the saintly women arrive, and they smile at me because they know they are about to bless me with their divine gifts. I love these women. They've become members of our family in some ways. Morgan usually invites them to stay for dinner, but they always decline. I bake them cookies sometimes, and they know they can drink all my coffee if they want to, because there is nothing we wouldn't do to try to bless them back.

The immaculate house has such a strange effect on my children. They say things like, "I just love it when the house is clean," and "I wish the house could be like this every day."

I scowl at them and reply, "Um. . .all we have to do is clean up after ourselves, and it could stay like this *all the time.*"

They clearly don't believe me, though, because twenty-four hours after the house is pristine and perfect, La Croix cans litter the upstairs game room and the bathroom trash can is full of a foreign substance I can't identify. You may think I'm exaggerating, but I can promise you that we once found maggots in my kids' bathroom trash can. I'll now give you a minute to vomit and then we'll get back to the Jesus stuff.

Actually, wait. Let's talk more about maggots.

WWJDAM: WHAT WOULD JESUS DO ABOUT MAGGOTS?

What are maggots, really, except reminders to all of us that mess and filth know no societal or cultural bounds? Anyone's trash cans are capable of becoming cesspools of foulness. God knows this is true about humans as well. The Bible proves God is fully aware that we are all quite ripe with rottenness. Consider this familiar passage from Isaiah 64:

> *We have all become like one who is unclean, and all our righteous deeds are like a polluted garment. We all fade like a leaf, and our iniquities, like the wind, take us away. There is no one who calls upon your name, who rouses himself to take hold of you; for you have hidden your face from us, and have made us melt in the hand of our iniquities.*
>
> *But now, O LORD, you are our Father; we are the clay, and you are our potter; we are all the work of your hand. (vv. 6–8 ESV)*

The bad news about everything in life is we're full of sin and stains, and cleaning ourselves up is beyond the scope of our ability. The good news is God made us, He loves us, and He's not cynical about us at all. In fact, He's pretty confident about His ability to fix everything.

I wonder what the world would look like if more of us walked around every week remembering that we bring with us our own maggot-like mess. What if we greeted everyone knowing we're all wet clay in the Father's hand—that basically, we're just God's favorite kind of dirt to make stuff out of? What if we attended church just grateful to have been given one more day to stand and sing praise to the God who is smoothing out all the imperfections in us as individuals and as a larger community?

What if we stopped looking for all the ways others' trash cans are full of maggots and chose to hold our hands very still before God, clinging to one another for stability? If this way of being in the world sounds familiar, it's because I got it from Jesus, who faced more than His fair share of cynicism and betrayal. Let's consider one of the most famous examples. (Hint: It has to do with His disciple Peter.)

NO SURPRISE

Jesus knew His dear friend Peter would betray Him and predicted it at the Passover table. He knew that Peter would feel abandoned and disillusioned by the death of Jesus-Who-Is-Supposed-to-Be-the-Messiah. But Jesus also knew that the source of Peter's pain would not be Jesus' crucifixion; rather, Peter's pain would result from his own lack of perspective about what the Messiah had come to do.

Peter was looking for his life to be changed; but Jesus had come to change Peter's eternity.

We've all betrayed and denied Christ in our past. We've let cynicism trick us into believing the world will never change, that God has let us down, or that we are sure to fail again. But today the rooster is crowing, and the sound is meant to give us hope that maybe Jesus knew what He was talking about after all.

When Jesus restored Peter after the resurrection in John 21, He asked Peter three times if he loved Him. Every time, Peter insisted that he loved Jesus very much, and with each declaration of love, Jesus asked Peter to prove it by either feeding His lambs or tending His sheep. Then He gave Peter another prophecy:

> *"Truly, truly, I say to you, when you were young, you*
> *used to dress yourself and walk wherever you wanted, but*

when you are old, you will stretch out your hands, and another will dress you and carry you where you do not want to go." (This he said to show by what kind of death he was to glorify God.) And after saying this he said to him, "Follow me." (John 21:18–19 ESV)

The wood pallet in my eye is usually my belief that I am the center of my own world. It is the belief that I get to decide what happens to me in life, how vulnerable I will be, and which people or organizations have the power to affect my life for good or for evil. When I live out of that belief, I lose the plot of the Gospel. I forget that I died when I repented of my sin and that I have been raised to life in Christ. He wants my life to be passed out as food of hope to others who are as dependent on God for living water and bread of life as I am.

The antidote for the cynicism that results from the messiness of humanity in this world is sacrificial love and service. And we are the ones who are meant to offer it in our churches, our workplaces, our schools, our governments, and maybe even Target.

TARGET AND THE KINGDOM OF HEAVEN

When all my kids were still shorter than I am and very much in toy-buying mode, I would frequently do my grocery shopping at Target after church on Sundays. One such Sunday, before I shopped, I took the kids to the toy section/daycare area where I left the oldest in charge and pretended that would go well.[27]

Once all the items were checked off my nonexistent list,[28]

---

[27] When there is only one year between children, the oldest does not have as much influence and authority as you would expect. Mutiny is always a real possibility.

[28] I shop by feel. While this strategy isn't good for my budget, it's completely good for my lazy brain and for Target's market share, I assume.

I grabbed the kids and rolled up to the checkout with my mountain of groceries.[29] Then I wilted as the cashier bagged the vegetables with the eggs and a lamp. When the total cost appeared on the screen, my oldest son shouted the number out loud because he couldn't believe we had to pay *"that much money!"*

I died a little of embarrassment, but I also felt gratitude to have the money to live so luxuriously. After all, I had bought six kinds of cereal, three gallons of milk, all the fruit we wanted, meat, bread for days, and of course everything chocolate. I felt the full miracle of our soon-to-be-full pantry. This revelation only made it all the more stirring when we saw a mom and two small children in the parking lot holding a sign. WE HAVE NOTHING. PLEASE HELP.

After we gave them several bags of food, my kids and I talked during the drive home about the challenges that mother faced. One of my younger children said something that surprised me: "I think it must be easier to love God if you are poor."

"Why do you think that?" I asked.

"Because you need Him so much more. For, like, *everything*," he said.

It is often tempting to ignore the wisdom of children, but Jesus once said something similar in the Beatitudes. Luke 6 recounts His words as, "Blessed are you who are poor, for yours is the kingdom of God" (v. 20 ESV); while Matthew 5 says it like this: "Blessed are the poor in spirit, for theirs is the kingdom of heaven" (v. 3 ESV). No matter how you slice it, there's a connection between understanding God's kingdom ways and

---

[29] The Target employee's eyes revealed her true feelings of shock. She smiled on the outside, but in her heart she was screaming, "This is not actually a grocery store, lady."

being aware of our own neediness.

Our church has a fairly large homeless community who attend on Sundays. They are very poor, and they really do need God for everything. We seek to make space for them to be seen, loved, and protected. Amazing volunteers work to meet their physical and spiritual needs. While I don't think it's necessarily easier for a homeless person to love God, it is often easier for them to admit that loving God is not an easy thing to do in a world as broken as ours.

There is nowhere for my homeless friends to hide their poverty when they are surrounded by middle-class people. Unlike the ways that I am needy, their needs can't be covered by wood pallet walls, successful self-reliance, or a gritty cynicism about life. They need help. They need a ride to the DMV. They need a doctor's appointment, some headache medication, or a place to shower and wash their laundry. They need a community that is diverse, full of people who have the power to help them get the things they need, as well as people who know from personal experience how hard street life really can be.

The Kingdom of God looks like all of us, holding signs that say "We have nothing. Please help."

We need clear eyes, with no specks or logs to be found in them, so we won't look away when we pass the needy. In fact, we need to see them so we can see ourselves among them, and so we can see God pointing at the places He wants us to start passing out what He put in our bags.

I really hope we will do it. Don't you?

CHAPTER 7

Pretty Things and Their Ugly Cousins at Home

How Consumerism Can't Save You

One year during Lent, I nonchalantly decided to fast from online shopping.[30] I regretted this decision a hundred times a day for forty days. This slow Lenten death taught me that online shopping had become my modus operandi for dealing with my life.

Forgive me, Father, for being a lover of virtual shopping carts.

For example, while sitting at a middle-school basketball game one night, I remembered that I'd seen only three remaining individual-portioned bags of cheese puffs in the pantry that morning after the kids went to school. I estimated we were two days away from the hormonal teenage nuclear bomb of shrugging and complaining that always occurs when there are "no good chips left." To avoid this mushroom cloud of teenage angst, I opened up my Amazon app to order a

---

[30] Fasting is so weird. It's like, *Hmm. . .how can I better identify with the painful experience of the crucifixion? I know! I'll shoot deuces at Amazon for forty days!* #prollynotthesamethingjesuswentthrough

week's worth of snacks.[31]

But I was fasting from online shopping. I closed the app. The children would have to eat apple slices instead.

Later after the game, I walked into the laundry room to switch the loads and noticed that the dryer filter thing that catches all the lint had mysteriously broken in half. I would need to replace it, obviously, because in a worst-case scenario world, the house would catch on fire if the lint wasn't adequately removed from the dryer. This is important stuff. But *where* does one buy a new dryer filter thing for a seven-year-old dryer? I didn't know. What I did know was that I was one google search away from not just finding out but possessing it.

However, I was fasting. *Go ahead and burn my house down, Self-Afflicted Lenten Bondage.*

Then our whole family got the flu. We needed orange juice, chicken broth, some soda, and lots and lots of medicine, but we didn't want any of our friends to be exposed to our germfest. Truth be told, no one was knocking down our front door to spoon-feed us chicken and noodles; until our fevers broke, we were *pariahs*. Oh grocery delivery services, we love you so dearly.

Except, I was fasting, so we remained grocery deficient and joined our brother Job in his anguished lament: "Let the day perish on which I was born" (Job 3:3 ESV).

As an introvert who would like to never, ever leave her house for any reason, I find shopping in the internet age to be full of unspeakable joy and blessing. I often open my front door and slide in boxes and boxes of home goods, groceries, face wash, tools, clothes, and shoes. I am living in a fairy-tale

---

[31] When you're twelve years old, you have four inalienable rights: life, liberty, the pursuit of happiness, and an endless supply of individual bags of Doritos.

land of miracles and unicorns simply because it's possible to go days without encountering anyone but my own family and the occasional UPS driver.[32]

In contrast, fasting from internet shopping was like being dropped from a plane without a parachute into total darkness.

Jesus plainly told us once that His yoke is easy and His burden is light (Matthew 11:30). He probably wasn't really thinking about my shopping life when He said that two thousand years ago, but during my online shopping fast, it felt like He was using those words to provoke me. The load of my fast was not light, nor was it easy. I'm not trying to compare my suffering to Jesus', but the truth is this no-internet-shopping thing slowly wore me down until I required an hour alone in prayer, two coffees, and a pep talk in the bathroom mirror[33] just to get in my car and go to the sporting goods store for new cleats for my son.

I suppose that is as it should be. Lent should stretch you out as thin as you can get to help you remember that this one small area of sacrifice is a forty-day-long experiment in suffering.

But why do we Christians put ourselves in a test tube of spiritual discipline like this?

I suppose it's because the weight of life cannot be quantified. We are rarely fully prepared to carry it. We need to practice *carrying heavy things*, and spiritual disciplines are good for practice.

If I had to ballpark it, I would say life's heaviness feels

---

[32] Don't you love your UPS drivers? They're like Santa and Mr. Rogers all rolled into one person with magnificent calf muscles.

[33] In the world of self-pep talks, I'm a big fan of either the Stuart Smalley version ("You're good enough, you're smart enough, and doggone it, people like you") or the Leslie Knope version ("You are a beautiful, talented, brilliant, powerful musk ox").

like one bagamajillion tons of pure deadweight resting on your shoulders. Some weeks I wonder how we will make it from Sunday to Sunday without running away and never coming back.[34]

We face financial stresses, relational discord, and health problems. We feel the weight of good things, like change and growth, that can add to the heavy lifting. But we also live in a spiritual world, and we would be foolish to forget the weight of darkness woven into the fabric of our lives. We have an enemy of evil who seeks to devour us. His goal is to ruin the Bride of Christ one person at a time.

How do we walk by faith in a world so full of problems and pain?

Let's return once more to the time Jesus touched on the spiritual battle we all face by putting Simon Peter on blast in Luke 22:31–34 (ESV):

> *"Simon, Simon, behold, Satan demanded to have you, that he might sift you like wheat, but I have prayed for you that your faith may not fail. And when you have turned again, strengthen your brothers." Peter said to him, "Lord, I am ready to go with you both to prison and to death." Jesus said, "I tell you, Peter, the rooster will not crow this day, until you deny three times that you know me."*

Peter, of course, told Jesus there was nothing to worry about whatsoever. Jesus was his homeboy. Peter would never turn

---

[34] Some weeks I plan out how to run away and never come back. Then I trash the plan because it always requires that I homeschool my kids again, which they've refused to do many times because the massively flawed public school system is preferable to being with me all day. If you wonder if I'm taking this personally, I'm not, but it's an excellent card to play in the game called Guilt Trip. #knowyourstrengths

away. He was ready to *die* for Jesus!

Peter was nothing if not confident. I admire his determination, even as I acknowledge his lack of self-awareness. Peter clearly didn't know what he was about to face, but Jesus did. Jesus even had instructions for Peter once he processed through all the trauma coming his way: "And when you have turned again, strengthen your brothers" (v. 32 ESV).

I wish I could tell you that when Satan comes to sift me like wheat, I prove stronger than my brother Peter. But I don't want to lie to you. I have some favorite diversions when traumatic circumstances hit me unexpectedly. Usually, when I turn away from the fight, I turn toward pretty things.

A TRUE AMERICAN IDOL

As an American, I have been well advertised to all my life. I have been promised that new things will make me feel better about myself, my marriage, my kids, and everything else that is broken in the world. I have marinated for over forty years in this marketing soup our culture doles out every day. The steady diet of consumerism has had its effects on my soul. Besides, I'm an aesthetic person, and pretty things are like water in the desert for my thirsty heart.

I have to remind myself, though, that no store sells living water, and nothing exposes my spiritual thirst like good old-fashioned trials and tribulations. Jesus went to the garden and prayed all night after His real talk with Peter when the weight of darkness fell upon Him. I'm certain prayer ought to be the first place I run when I can't bear the burden of God's call to endure pain and loss for His kingdom.

Unfortunately, on my way to my prayer closet, I frequently browse the sale items at Anthropologie. My thirsty soul picks out something simple, like one small water glass to set by my bathroom sink. It's a pretty one, with gold and yellow Moroccan designs on it. I rationalize this purchase as *practical* because I will use it for drinking a glass of water every morning when I take my vitamins.

I also tell myself this purchase has nothing to do whatsoever with the despair rising up from my gut. Like Peter, I can easily deceive myself when necessary.

The glass costs eight dollars. But I pay hundreds, maybe thousands, for it with the currency my soul has scrimped and saved over the years. We pay our mortgages with hard cash, but every human on earth socks away trust and hope and courage to pay the deed on the promised land of internal peace. It's only when Satan comes to sift us that we realize we may not have *quite* enough to buy our way out; we will need our Father to pay the difference.

Then we get to decide all over again if we're going to go shopping or fall on our faces before God.

The next time I consider buying another shopping-therapy glass, that glass and I need to have a talk. Yes, I am the kind of person who will speak to a glass in a store. I will do it even when my daughter is with me, because she has her own Moroccan glass idols and I am trying to show her a better way to live. I'll stand there in Anthropologie and point my finger at the little water glass and tell it the truth: "You are a very, very pretty little thing. But you can't change my world like I want you to. You can't undo what's been done or save me from my fear. You're just made of sand and some paint. I have some other glasses at home that work just fine. Sure, they're not as pretty as you, but those ugly cousins of yours will hold my water the same way you can. And I know that if I walk away from you today, I will win a little more courage for my heart. Choosing to leave you here reminds me that my help comes from God Himself. So thank you for your beauty, but I'm afraid I already have everything I really need today in Jesus."

The first time my daughter heard me talk to the pretty things, she stared at me in disbelief. Then she smiled at me and said, "I didn't know you could do that."

You can too! *We all can do that.* When we're tempted to turn away from the Gospel's call to have faith in the midst of our pain and suffering by finding hope in some pretty things, we can pivot back to God instead.

PIVOT. PIVOT! *PIVOT!*

Now that I've used the word *pivot*, I am obligated to talk about the TV show *Friends*. I apologize for this deep dive into '90s TV culture,[35] but the pivot episode is unforgettable. The basic plot is that Ross bought a new sofa but refused to pay the delivery cost, so Ross, Chandler, and Rachel attempt to carry the sofa up a very narrow set of stairs in a New York City apartment building. The stairs make an abrupt turn to the right, and the harder they try to jam the sofa around the corner, they more they realize Ross' dream of getting it in his apartment is impossible.

Ross is really calm at first, but the more inept Rachel and Chandler become at lifting that sofa, the more frustrated and angry Ross gets. He starts shouting at them, "Pivot. Pivot. *Pivot!*"

By the end of the show, the sofa is cut in two pieces and

---

[35] Even though the show is full of flaws, lacks diversity of any kind, and is entirely unrealistic, it endures as a fantastical dreamland of sorts. Oh to be young, surrounded by friends who love you, and live in a massive New York apartment with rent control. It's the American dream.

ripped to shreds because they forced it up those stairs. In a hilarious final visit to the furniture store, Ross tries to return the two pieces of the broken sofa because he isn't "satisfied with it." The saleswoman gives him four dollars of store credit for the demolished couch.

This scene begs the question: How many times are we going to empty our bank accounts and break our souls in pieces trying to get ourselves up the stairwell of life when Jesus already paid a steep price to deliver God's people safe and whole right to the Father Himself?

If you don't pivot back toward God and beg for mercy when consumerism offers you a fictitious kind of salvation through pretty things, then a pretty glass by your bathroom sink could lead to a whole fantasy redo of your bathroom in a Moroccan theme. Instead of dealing with the real problems you face and cultivating faith and hope in your soul, you could easily spend at least three weeks researching new paint colors, light fixtures, and tile choices that would accentuate your new glass quite nicely. Eventually, you may be forced to admit you can't afford a Moroccan bathroom, but if you're still quite set on being distracted from your neediness when that happens, the new Pottery Barn catalog will arrive, and you will temporarily eschew your troubles by browsing their new line of bedding.

Or you could pivot back to the Gospel and endure the discomfort of your spiritual stairwell. You could risk looking foolish by believing that God will do miraculous things because He already promised to carry you home Himself.

Paul wrote that this narrow spiritual stairwell of ours leads to "What no eye has seen, nor ear heard, nor the heart of man imagined, what God has prepared for those who love him" (1

Corinthians 2:9 ESV). Every pretty thing becomes dull when placed next to the incomprehensibly beautiful plans God has for us. The Holy Spirit will reveal it all to us—if we will sit faithfully in the stairwell long enough.

Owning things is not our fundamental purpose in life. We know this cognitively, and yet we live as if our possessions define us. We say things like, "I always get the new phone when it releases. It's my thing. It's kind of who I am," or "I saw that shirt, and I had to have it—it was so 'me,'" or "This apartment doesn't really communicate who I am." *Of course an inanimate object doesn't communicate who you are.* You are a spiritual being who will live for eternity, who was so beloved by God that He sent His Son to die so you could live with Him forever. No one phone/shirt/apartment can adequately proclaim the brilliance of your existence.

You are Holy Guacamole. Holy Guacamole isn't an off-the-rack purchase. God didn't snag you on a Black Friday deal that included free shipping. You were expensive, and God never wants you to believe that some pretty thing increases your belovedness or significance. Stuff is just stuff, after all, while you are spiritual treasure hidden in a human body. You're the lost coin He sought through blood and tears. You're the lamb He journeyed long and hard to bring back to the flock; the prodigal child God watched for with great anticipation; the one He ran to welcome home so He could plan the greatest party in history.

You are more precious and valuable than you can ever imagine.

We take none of our pretty things (or their ugly cousins, thank the Lord in heaven for that) with us when we leave this life for eternity. But learning to hold them more loosely is exceptionally challenging for many of us. If we will make a practice of refusing to link our identity with our possessions, though, holding them loosely can empower us to be generous in the way God designed.

Late one December 25 night, after all the packages had been unwrapped and all the cinnamon rolls and ham and candy canes had been devoured, my teenage son called me upstairs to help him use the gift card his grandmother had given him to buy some shoes online. We sat curled up on his bed with the computer, looking at basketball shoes with famous players' names attached to them. This child of mine likes flashy, expensive shoes, and he was in sneakerhead heaven, holding his golden ticket to a new pair of kicks.

The challenge we faced was that he didn't have enough money on that gift card for the shoes he wanted most of all. These shoes cost as much as our electric bill in the Texas August heat, and I had to admire his determination when he pulled out his wallet and counted up all the money he had earned from babysitting and doing chores. He was still short ten dollars.

"I get my allowance in a week. Can I have it early?"

I was so tempted to hand over the money. After a long day of open hands to this child, one more moment of pure joy on his face would have felt like winning. But a small check in my heart told me I needed to ask him a question first.

"Have you tithed on what you've earned already?"

"Oh. . .no. But I can do that in January too."

I thought about all the presents piled up for him downstairs: the games and books and clothes and super-amazing basketball shoes he had already opened that morning. I decided to refuse him next month's money.[36]

"I'm sorry, bud. I think your options are to buy a cheaper pair of shoes or wait until you get your allowance next week to shop," I said.

The words scraped my throat as I spoke them. My son's disappointment was palpable. After the delicious taste of getting everything he could possibly want all day, the bitterness of *no* was a bit of a shock to his system. A giant cup of consumerism had been served up for us all that day, and the best antidote for its intoxicating taste was this two-letter word. I promised him we would go to the outlet mall to see if he could find something there, and he agreed that might be a better choice.

"But I just want those shoes *so bad*," he said.

"Well, you can buy them next week when you have more money if you don't find something cheaper that you like just as much."

But of course, as all good lessons in life go, he did find something better at the outlet. He found a pair of ridiculously expensive basketball shoes on the clearance rack for forty dollars—which was a fraction of what he had tried to spend. In a small way, it was like discovering grace and gratitude in a box. After he finished exulting over his killer kicks, I wandered through the women's clearance rack and found a pair of shoes I had wanted for months. I decided to give myself a dose of my own medicine and put them back on the shelf. But that kid of mine wouldn't let me. The boy who'd asked to borrow

---

[36] I blame this Grinch-worthy behavior on the fact that I am a cruel, heartless mother who values her child's depth of character above his momentary happiness. #hohoho #nonono #Godblessuseveryone

money two days before offered to pay for part of my shoes.

"I never got you a Christmas present, so this can be from me!" Mr. Big Bucks said.

Then his brother next to him coughed up more money toward my shoes. I sat in the outlet mall in awe of my kids as they begged me to take some of the money they had planned to spend on themselves.

Now, of course, Jesus didn't die so we could find better deals at the outlets. However, in the middle of the ordinary choices we make, such as how much to spend on a pair of shoes or when to splurge on an eight-dollar glass, there lies a deeper story about a God who has already given us all we could ever need.[37]

IN DEEP WATER

The first step away from consumerism and greed is usually the most painful because it's a choice to refuse to worship the idol of pretty things. This idolatry is a particularly influential force in the world because God created beauty to set the human heart ablaze. Beauty is meant to draw us to God. One minute we're wading around in tide pools and the next minute the beauty of wild ocean surf crashing on rocks pulls us out of ourselves and into the deep water of experiencing the divine. This can happen to us while viewing a beloved masterpiece in person or gazing upon a newborn child or grandchild. Many of the Psalms express this truth, showing how beauty in the world draws the human heart toward something greater.

For all the gods of the peoples are worthless idols, but the
LORD made the heavens. Splendor and majesty are before

---

[37] Jesus is ever with us, but He is especially noticeable in the clearance section. Except at the Lululemon outlet; they never have my size, and the Spirit is quenched within me every time.

him; strength and beauty are in his sanctuary. Ascribe to
the LORD, O families of the peoples, ascribe to the LORD
glory and strength! (Psalm 96:5–7 ESV)

People have been replicating, recreating, reinventing, and mir-
roring beauty for millennia. We can't seem to help it. In her
book *On Beauty and Being Just*, Elaine Scarry describes how
beholding a beautiful thing creates a need in people to create more beauty.[1] The narrative of beauty could go like this: a
woman sees a sunset, so she writes a poem about its vibrant
colors, which is read by a boy who makes a gorgeous kite of
those colors and flies it in the sky. His father sees the kite and
is mesmerized by the beauty of how it soars, so he finds his
wife and dances with her beneath it. The wife is caught up
in the beauty of her husband's joy, and it presses her to take
a bouquet of flowers to a suffering friend. The bouquet is so
pretty that her friend paints a picture of it and sells it. She
gives the money to a nonprofit in her community that orga-
nizes art programs in schools. On and on beauty goes, propel-
ling the beholders of it along and leaving acts of fairness and
justice and more beauty in its wake.

Scarry goes on in her book to explain that just as beauty
compels us to create more beauty, it also causes us to seek the
divine as our minds try to find the source of the beauty we
behold.[2] She argues that this transcendent experience with
the beginning of all beauty reminds us of the abstract laws and
principles of justice in the world. Therefore, beholding beautiful things inspires us to create justice.

Given Scarry's analysis, gathering up all the pretty things
could be our attempt to plug into the powerful force of
beauty so we can overcome the brutal facts about our current

circumstances and possibly be catapulted into a fairer future.

Perhaps, though, to find our way to a more just and beautiful future, we also need to remember the beauty and justice of the past. Like the spiritual discipline of fasting, remembering takes practice and sacrifice, because we have to let go of our grip on our fear and our worries so we can hold the memories of how God led us to where we are now.

I REMEMBER

Long before I was shopping for pretty things on my own, I was a seven-year-old little girl who loved spending the day at the beach with her mom. I remember digging for hermit crabs in the sandy bubbles and collecting them in a bright orange sand bucket; eating peanut butter sandwiches and fat green grapes laced with a few grains of sand; and drinking sweet juice from an old red plaid thermos.

I remember one day in particular that began with all these things. The sun was high but not too hot, the beach wasn't too crowded, and the Pacific's tide was calm and serene, so Mom and I decided to take a swim. We ventured out almost to the buoys. I can still remember how my body effortlessly rose over and beyond the gentle swells of water heading for shore. The seagulls cried out overhead, and the water tasted salty in my mouth. It was thrilling and a little frightening to have unknown depths of sea beneath me.

But the tide suddenly changed once we were out in the deep water. My mom and I treaded water as the waves passed us and grew tall and fierce, moving closer to the beach and eventually crashing on the shore with weighty, massive roars.

There would be no leisurely body surfing back to the beach. We would have to swim back under looming white water.

I was very, very scared.[38] I wished we had never swum out so far. A man we didn't know swam over and offered to help me to the shore, but that terrified me even more, so we declined.

Several times, we began toward the beach only to have to swim back out into the deep water, because a wave was breaking over us and our timing was terrible. Eventually, we put our heads down and took on the beastly waves, swimming furiously. In the end, we made it safely to dry ground.

My last memory of that day is of standing on the shore wrapped in my beach towel. The afternoon sun had dropped over the horizon, and I was mesmerized by the beauty and power of the ocean surf. I felt a new respect for the mighty Pacific and a triumphant joy that we had done such a hard thing. I know now that I was experiencing what Elaine Scarry writes about, what God planned from the very beginning when He created all that exists and called it good.

It's essential for me to remember that day, because life often sends waves that crash over me in frightening ways, and I always wish I could be anywhere except right where darkness looms and threatens to take me under. When the going gets tough, I want to quit. But then I stop and remember.

When I really and truly need saving, I don't remember how good it feels to bring home a pretty new sweater from the mall. I don't remember how fun it is to choose a new sofa or to set the table with beautiful dishes. I don't pick up my new earrings and hold them until I feel brave enough to trust God.

I remember that I was made to be a person who swims for solid ground, even when she's scared. I remember that even when I can't see God in the terrifying waves of my circumstances, He is always there with me. I don't need to hold a

---

[38] I didn't know it then, but my mom was afraid too. She handled it like a champ.

pretty thing; I need to pick up a piece of bread and a tiny cup of juice so I can commune with God and remember His words:

> *And he took bread, and when he had given thanks, he broke it and gave it to them, saying, "This is my body, which is given for you. Do this in remembrance of me." And likewise the cup after they had eaten, saying, "This cup that is poured out for you is the new covenant in my blood." (Luke 22:19–20 ESV)*

Jesus knew that our taste and our memory are linked in mysterious ways in our brains. Long before consumerism was a way of life in a capitalistic society, Jesus knew we would long to consume something that could help us believe salvation is real and is for us. He knew that when His followers no longer had Him standing there in front of them, they would need a physical thing to touch and hold that would remind them of what He was about to do on the cross. Jesus knew a familiar food could transport us back to a specific moment in time. He knew gritty grapes and sweet juice would take me back to the beach.

When the going gets tough and life seems too heavy with darkness, Jesus offered us a kind of love and rest humans have traveled the world to find. It's ours for the remembering and the holding in a simple taste of bread and wine.

It's good for us to remember and feel our deep need for salvation. It's good for us to consider all the ways we could try to save ourselves with pretty things, perfection, knowledge, or any of the other things we discuss in these chapters. It's good for us to choose instead to remember the cross and pivot toward God. And someday, when we arrive at His throne, we will see that it was always His goodness that kept us afloat on all the long, hard days we thought might consume us.

May we never stop swimming until we reach the shore of this promise to us:

Keep your life free from love of money, and be content with what you have, for he has said, "I will never leave you nor forsake you." So we can confidently say, "The Lord is my helper; I will not fear; what can man do to me?" (Hebrews 13:5–6 ESV)

CHAPTER 8

GOD'S WILL IS LIKE A CHARCUTERIE BOARD

How Doubting God's Love Can't Save You

I JUST DON'T WANT TO LOOK BACK AND THINK,
I COULD HAVE EATEN THAT.
UNKNOWN

In our house, we have some picky eaters. One of the picky eaters doesn't like being called a "picky eater" and would prefer to be called something like "an eater with a discerning palate."

Shall we just shorten that to EDP? Yes, we shall.

My EDPs have clear boundaries in regard to what they absolutely will not eat. Four of them refuse bananas of any kind. One won't allow a fruit other than apples to pass his lips.[39] There is an EDP in my family who thinks most pasta and every form of rice are abhorrent entirely, and another whose violent, primal reaction to brussels sprouts borders on a convulsive seizure. One EDP thinks peaches are divine—except for the fuzzy skin, which could clearly be used by the government to force traitorous double agent spies to confess their secrets.

There are also clear boundaries about what my EDPs will

---

[39] I once offered this person twenty dollars to lick a strawberry. He couldn't do it. Tears were shed. He wanted that twenty bucks so bad, but alas, the strawberry was far too intimidating. This proves what we've always suspected: strawberries are the mean bullies of the fruit world. #sweettormentor

eat. Homemade desserts are, of course, a divine right in life, but if store-bought cookies are forced upon them, Oreos and Chips Ahoy! are the only acceptable options.[40] In the category of chips, baked sour cream and cheddar potato chips are preferred over the regular fried version, and a bag of blue Doritos outranks the red bag by a million votes.

Some of you are thinking I have allowed too much leniency in food preferences, which has resulted in raising children who are obstinate and opinionated about the food for which they merely ought to be grateful.

I can see your line of reasoning. My failure is quite complete in this area. For example, I didn't "make" them eat spinach enough as toddlers. However, I'm not sure how one "makes" toddlers eat anything without sitting on top of them and smashing the food into their faces. Grace compels me to be a bit subtler in my parenting.

In my defense, not all of the EDPs in our family are children. I don't want to expose the vulnerability of anyone who lives in our house, but if you invite us to dinner, please don't serve a certain patriarchal person bananas wrapped in the skin of a peach as an appetizer.[41]

As you can probably imagine, planning meals is complicated since every meal involves feeding several people who seem to be genetically predisposed to disdain a variety of foods. Being the true sacrificial martyr that I am, I generally suffer in silence as I serve tacos and spaghetti again. But some nights I unapologetically dish up a soup that involves strange

---

[40] One exception to this rule happens during the time of year when those cute Girl Scouts hawk their boxes of deliciousness, in which case we need twenty boxes of Thin Mints to ensure our survival.

[41] Or mushrooms, mayonnaise, ranch dressing, eggs that are not scrambled, or any sour cream-based sauce. Actually, just don't invite us to dinner. We'll have you over instead. It's easier that way.

vegetables, such as leeks and kale. I personally love and appreciate these ingredients as nutrient-rich sources of sustenance, and the medley of offended people at the table are invited to just suck it up and eat what I ladle out to them.

Because sometimes in life, you get what you get.

YOU CAN'T ALWAYS GET WHAT YOU WANT

Of course, "You get what you get" doesn't only apply to our available food sources. From our first breath, there are realities about our lives we do not choose, which we have no power to change or control. You didn't select the nation you were born in, the color of your skin, the height of your body, the coarseness of your hair, the muscular structure of your legs, or the natural talent you possess in any given area of life. We don't get to choose whether the homes of our childhoods are safe or unsafe, nor can we select the level of trauma we are exposed to by either evil people or evil social structures. We can't force life to give us privileges like a neighborhood full of awesome kids to play with after school or parents who are able to pay for tutoring when Algebra 2 is knocking us flat. We can't undo our genetic predispositions. We can't coerce from life picture-perfect features.

The unfairness of our existence is astounding when we consider the broadness of all the circumstances over which we have no control.

Those who see the universe as random may find it easier to accept the cruel realities of life. For such people, there is no one to blame for our cosmic insignificance, but also nowhere to place our hope for redemption. With no higher power or divine guide, we all get what we get, and that's kind of. . .it.

But for those of us who have believed the Christian

message that God loves us and desires to bless us, how do we come to the table in life and muster up the courage to accept a meal that is sour and strange to us? How do we eat the bitter circumstances God lays before us without doubting either the veracity of God's love or our own value?

Put simply, at some point in life unjust and cruel hardships cause even the sincerest followers of Jesus to wrestle with the big question of "Why?" Why do bad things happen to people who love God and are loved by God? Why didn't God spare us from tragedy? Why must we suffer?

In our attempt to answer this deep soul question, there are two well-worn, albeit dysfunctional and unwise, paths forward. Our first option is to moralize suffering and say that there must be some kind of fault on the part of the one who suffers. The law of sowing and reaping supports this idea, as did the theology of the Pharisees of Jesus' time.[42] Many Christians believe this in subtle ways by assuming that hardships, disease, and even poverty are the natural result of sins such as a lack of faith, laziness, or simply poor character. After all, they reason, people who work hard, pray enough, take good care of themselves and their families, and love God can naturally avoid all sorts of sad circumstances like job loss, a bad diagnosis, and wayward children. This path is attractive to our human desire to be in control because it promises us we can protect ourselves from suffering by being very, very good and diligent people.

The second easy path forward when we doubt God's will is to denigrate God's love for us either because He is not the good God we once believed He is or because we are not

---

[42] See John 9 for how Jesus proved the moralistic solution is not always applicable. #teamjesus #forgodsglory

actually worthy enough to receive good things from Him. In that case, our suffering is, in part, our own fault—we realize we never should have trusted God in the first place. Our souls are hypnotized by the desire to protect ourselves from suffering by refusing to be bamboozled by the hope for divine help in the future. God can't let us down if we refuse to trust Him.

There is a third path forward, and while it is less dysfunctional, it is also not particularly smooth and attractive. Jesus would have called it narrow, and He would like us all to know it leads to life. I like to call it the Switchbacks of Death.

RUN, JESUS, RUN

When I was a young whippersnapper of a girl at Canyon High School, I ran cross-country. Every season, we ran several races at Mt. San Antonio College (aka Mt. SAC) in Walnut, California. The three-mile racecourse there is a harrowing combination of hilly terrain and long, dry, hot paths through what feels like a desert of doom. Portions of the course named "Valley Loop," "Poop-out Hill," and "Reservoir Hill" have become part of cross-country legend, and the course is quite famous around the world.

The first gauntlet in the race, a path called the "Switchbacks," still stands out in my memory. After the gun would go off, every runner would enjoy a quick quarter-mile approach to a hill so steep that we had to cut it in sharp turns right and then left and then back again and again. We couldn't have possibly run straight up this hill. We could barely run up it as it was. I passed many runners in my races over the years who looked like they were walking up the Switchbacks because they couldn't initiate any forward motion on the incline. Once we got to the downhill portion, our legs were like wet noodles, and we faced the incredibly sad fact that even though we had only just begun the race, we were dead already.

No one should ever have to run this race. We ran it three times every year. In fact, our regional races were all run there. If we wanted to qualify for the state meet, we had to win at Mt. SAC. Our success as a team or as individuals hinged upon running this course well.

How did we survive?

For those grueling twenty minutes, our minds focused only on how it would feel to cross the finish line victorious. Every person we passed was one more person who would have to suffer longer than we would, and therefore we tried to pass every person we could. We just wanted the race over as quickly as possible. We savored the future taste of that holy moment when we could exult in the glory of knowing we were among the special, set-apart athletes who had once again conquered Mt. SAC.

I didn't know Jesus when I was in high school. I hadn't learned yet how many times the New Testament compares our faith to running a race. But now I know that by running those races I was unwittingly practicing the spiritual discipline of endurance—even when the path ahead looks like the Switchbacks of Death. I was learning to press on toward the finish line, to take even the narrowest, steepest path and eat the bitter pain life serves me.

The race is unfair and tough to run. Trusting you will find God on the Switchbacks of Death is the third path you can take to try to answer the question of why so many bad things happen in life. It's a somewhat grueling hill that leads up to the table of God, where, if you eat what God serves, you will find the hidden holiness in the Holy Guacamole of His will.

HIDDEN HOLINESS

Hidden all around us is God's holy will. It is hidden in our relationships with people who are hard to love, and it's in people who love us so well that we can hardly believe they're real. It's hidden in long nights nursing the sick and in longer days entering data on a computer so that we can provide for our families. God's holy will is woven into every conflict facing us, and it's in every peaceful reconciliation. God's holiness is packaged beautifully in our anger when justice seems to have been forgotten by those in power and in our longing for the next generation to experience a world with less suffering and more safe places. The blessing of redemption has always been God's plan for the world, and if we are disheartened by the lack of redemption we see in the world, it's possible we need to take a closer look at how God's best redemptive work progressed through the ages.

We can see how God's will was hidden in plain sight in Jesus. With the well-developed teachings of centuries of theologians in our back pocket, it's astounding to fathom how the disciples could not conceive that God had sent a Savior who would be executed by the government to overthrow the reign of sin in our world. It seems so obvious on this side of church history and doctrine. However, no matter how many times Jesus taught about laying down one's life for one's friends (John 15:13), told parables about seeds dying (John 12:24), and said that to find your life you first have to lose it (Matthew 10:39)—not to mention He literally told His followers that He would have to die—the disciples were utterly stunned by the turn of events that preceded the crucifixion.

Seeing God's holiness in the crucifixion was impossible for the disciples. Kind of like seeing God's holiness in the suffering in our lives and in the lives of the people we love is often impossible for us now.

Like us, the original followers of Jesus made assumptions about how God was going to save them. Like us, they assumed the Messiah was there to save them from the things that hounded them and kept them up at night.[43] Like us, they applied their limited understanding of God's will to their circumstances and came up with an often shortsighted vision of what God really had planned.

God's plans are always broader and deeper and more complex than we expect because His end goal is not to bless us only for today. God's end goal is to bless the whole world by leading His people into a more profound call to love and obey Him.

In fact, that's precisely what the will of God has been working for centuries to produce in the earth. After His resurrection, Jesus explained to the disciples how the Jewish scriptures, the writings Christians now call the Old Testament, all explain God's deepest dream, namely, the promise of salvation and blessing for the world. We can see it clearly when we look at the original promise God gave to Abraham:

> *"I will make you into a great nation, and I will bless you;*
> *I will make your name great, and you will be a blessing.*
> *I will bless those who bless you, and whoever curses you I*
> *will curse; and all peoples on earth will be blessed through*
> *you." (Genesis 12:2–3 NIV)*

---

[43] For the disciples, this was most likely the oppressive government rule they were under. For many of us in first world nations, it's something more like our unjust bosses or whether we will be able to afford to pay for our kids to go to college. I feel like we have it a smidgeon easier in life than they did. But we shouldn't think about that for too long, or our pity parties will become terribly dull, you know?

God promised Abraham that He would bless him. But God didn't stop with blessing Abraham alone. God started pointing at everyone in the future and shouting, *"You get a blessing! You get a blessing! And* you *get a blessing!"* in much the same way Oprah would pass out cars to her audience thousands of years later.[44] This is the first glimpse we have of the good news that God planned to send a Messiah. Paul saw it clearly and alluded to it when he wrote, "Scripture foresaw that God would justify the Gentiles by faith, and announced the gospel in advance to Abraham: 'All nations will be blessed through you'" (Galatians 3:8 NIV).

Paul then emboldened Christ-followers to be like our spiritual father Abraham. "So those who rely on faith are blessed along with Abraham, the man of faith" (v. 9 NIV). And how, exactly, did Abraham live out his faith? Well, first he obeyed God by leaving the safety of his home and seeking a land God would show him. Abraham prioritized his relationship with God over the values of his family-centric culture, trusting Him completely. Abraham took the mysterious meal God served him, and he ate it in faith. He had no scriptures to read as encouragement, no church leaders to cheer him on up the steep hills of homelessness and infertility. Abraham just chewed and swallowed and trusted God would one day bless him and all peoples of the world.

As a result, we've all been blessed.

Abraham's story causes me to wonder about several things. First, how many beloved people of God throughout history had to choose to obey God and eat bitter circumstances while

---

[44] Generosity wasn't invented by wealthy people who like a nice fat tax deduction. It originated in the heart of God and His desire to bless all that He created. Unlike every human philanthropist, God gets no monetary kickback or benefit from all He gives us. He gives because He loves, and He loves because He is love.

clinging to their trust in God's goodness just so you and I could one day hear the Gospel? Second, how many generations ahead of us will be impacted by our choice to trust that even on the darkest days, God is working to bring about His most beautiful plans of blessing in the world? In many ways, we get what we get in life. But no matter what difficulties life serves us, obeying God means living in the promise He gave Abraham and trusting that God has good plans for us all.

But even when our hearts are full of Gospel faith, it can be hard to get some of the food God serves us down without a gag reflex kicking into gear. Some flavors are more complex and frightening than others.

SCARY FOOD

A few years ago, a friend of ours gave us a gift certificate to a restaurant with a menu that can only be described as "experimental cuisine." I've gone into great detail about the EDP nature of my family, so it shouldn't surprise you that when I looked up the restaurant online, I laughed. I could have warned my husband about the horrors that awaited him at this particular restaurant, but alas, I am a cruel woman who occasionally enjoys watching her generally confident husband squirm a little, so I zipped my lip and booked a reservation.

I'm not so heartless that I didn't at least give him a tiny heads-up that we were in for an adventure. Once we were en route to the restaurant, I casually mentioned, "The menu for this place is really different. The descriptions of the dishes don't really seem to be written in English."

Morgan assured me that our friends knew us *very* well. They wouldn't send us there if it wasn't the kind of place we would like. After all, they *love us*, he declared.

Famous last words.

I have no idea what we ate that night. I do know that I had to taste every single dish our servers brought us first to tell Morgan if he could stomach it or not. The most bizarre thing we consumed involved plastic medical syringes used as a kind of skewer for some sort of mostly raw meat and vegetable concoction. To eat this dish, you inserted the syringe in your mouth and pulled the meat off with your teeth while simultaneously dispensing tangy sauce onto your tongue. We learned several things that night:

1. Our friends *don't* know us very well.
2. Our friends *would* send us to a restaurant we would hate.
3. Our friends *may not* love us that much after all.
4. It's physically impossible for me to stop laughing at Morgan when he is terrified of the scary food on his plate.
5. When you feel a little ill from your experimental cuisine experience, a quick drive-through hamburger can fix everything.

But the uncomfortable experience of eating at that restaurant brought to mind the now-familiar-to-me strangeness of Jesus' words in John 6:53–58 (ESV):

> "*Truly, truly, I say to you, unless you eat the flesh of the Son of Man and drink his blood, you have no life in you. Whoever feeds on my flesh and drinks my blood has eternal life, and I will raise him up on the last day. For my flesh is true food, and my blood is true drink. Whoever*

*feeds on my flesh and drinks my blood abides in me, and
I in him. As the living Father sent me, and I live because
of the Father, so whoever feeds on me, he also will live
because of me. This is the bread that came down from
heaven, not like the bread the fathers ate, and died. Whoever feeds on this bread will live forever."*

The same way our friends missed the potential impact of
strange food on an EDP, we can read these words and miss
how bizarre they could sound to someone unfamiliar with the
basic foundational teachings of thousands of years of church
history. God's promise to Abraham sounded so simple and
straightforward. Why did Jesus have to make it so weird
and complicated? If I told you to eat my flesh and drink my
blood so you could abide in me, you would wisely stop reading my book right now.[45]

But I would never tell you to do that. I will, however, tell
you what to eat on Christmas Eve.

For our family, Christmas Eve dinner has always been a
bit of a challenge. Our church always has several services on
Christmas Eve, and planning a meal for after these services is
not a simple task. We're gone most of the day, and I don't want
to have to clean up a big cooking mess. One year I refused to
plan at all, and our family ended up driving all over town late
at night on December 24, looking for a restaurant that was still
open. Spoiler alert for all Austinites who try this in the future:
there isn't one.

The next year, Morgan suggested we do a simple cheese
and crackers kind of spread. I knew what he was imagining:
some cut-up fruit and vegetables laid out with Ritz crackers

---

[45] Please don't stop reading my book right now.

and slices of cheddar, Monterey Jack, and maybe a jalapeno cheese if we were really getting fancy.

But like Jesus, I had to make it weird. I used the power of Pinterest to completely overdo the cheese and crackers idea. I searched for two weeks for charcuterie board inspiration, and the resulting Christmas glory was magnificent. I had eight kinds of cheese and an equal variety of crackers. I laid out fresh fruit, dried fruit, a medley of olives, and a little jar of honey. I sliced a baguette into little round gluten bits of love and lined them up next to cured meats and salty cheeses. I opened jars of fig jam and raspberry chipotle sauce and put mother-of-pearl knives in them. I scattered roasted nuts and little blocks of chocolate around like confetti at a five-year-old's birthday party.

It was the best meal we had all year.

All the boring EDPs in the house started with whatever they wanted (namely, the Ritz crackers, apple slices, cheddar cheese, and chocolate bars). But then they began to get a little something sweet along with something salty, inventing combinations they had never dared eat before. I was so proud of them. As I wrapped a piece of prosciutto around a date stuffed with parmesan cheese, I thought a lot about how the sweet and the bitter mingle together to make something more deliciously complex. Then I popped a kalamata olive in my mouth, and I rediscovered my ability to taste all over again.

I remembered then, with sincere gratitude, a time in my life several years before when the steepness of the path God had asked me to take caused me to doubt everything. I doubted my ability to finish the race. I questioned whether God's love was for me. I doubted holiness could be hidden in the taste of trauma and pain. It all culminated in one moment that involved me on the floor of my kitchen mopping up soap suds after one of my kids had unwittingly used dish soap in the dishwasher, causing a flood in our house. There on my hands and knees, I began shouting the words of Proverbs 27:7 (ESV): "One who is full loathes honey, but to one who is hungry everything bitter is sweet."

I was so incredibly hungry during that time. I was hungry for reconciliation and redemption. My very broken heart wanted to take the familiar worldly path of blame and self-salvation. I longed to run away and refuse to eat one more bitter thing on the plate in front of me. But the Spirit of God within me compelled me to open my mouth and take in all the pain as sustenance of some kind. God asked me that day, *"Will you eat the bitter things even when they seem too scary or complex to be good for you?"*

Would I? I wasn't sure I *could.* Could I eat the flesh of Christ and drink His blood? Could I muster the courage to trust that my obedience to God would result in a blessing—not only for my current circumstance but with consideration to His original promise to Abraham? Could Galatians 3:9 mean that my steadfast faith could help carry the good news to all peoples of the earth?

I don't know how you will answer this question when it comes to you. But I know that I just said yes to it all. I would be brave. I would eat scary things. I could, and I would refuse to run away or take an easier way out. I mopped up the flood that day and forgave the child. In the following weeks and months, I answered the emails about all the problems. I prayed for the people I knew who were in distress. I chose to believe the best when I wanted to blame others for the worst. I sowed my money, my time, my heart, and my effort into the places God pointed at and said, *"This is the land I've led you to. Make a difference there."*

I didn't do it perfectly. I may get to heaven and find out that I missed something, somewhere. But there were a few times I found that eating conflict and misunderstanding and failure while trusting God brought me a kind of peace I never knew existed here on earth.

John 3:16–17 (esv) familiarly says, "For God so loved the world, that he gave his only Son, that whoever believes in him should not perish but have eternal life. For God did not send his Son into the world to condemn the world, but in order that the world might be saved through him." The reason the sacrifice of Jesus was so powerful is that He was so incredibly valuable. As one person of the triune God, as the beginning and the end of all things, as the Word of God made flesh—this Jesus of ours is priceless and irreplaceable in every possible way. When we allow ourselves to be sacrificed for the sake of His purpose, to be sown into His kingdom as seeds that have died in the ground and rely on Him to give them life, we become holy like Him, priceless like Him, irreplaceable pieces of God's grand plan to bless all the peoples of the world.

A Holy Guacamole life looks like obedience and faithfulness to run to God and eat whatever He serves us without doubting His love.

For God so loved you and me that He sent Himself so we too could be blessed and be sent as a blessing. Who doesn't want to eat that?

CHAPTER 9

HOUSTON, WE HAVE A PROBLEM
How Success Can't Save You

SOMETIMES YOU JUST HAVE TO PUT ON LIP
GLOSS AND PRETEND TO BE PSYCHED.
MINDY KALING[1]

Four years ago, I was smack in the middle of a very quiet season with God. Well, to be fair, *I* wasn't the one being quiet. I was complaining and crying and telling God how angry I was about some circumstances in my life and in the lives of my friends and family.

God held His tongue, though. It took me two years to be done accosting Him every time I prayed. Once I had run out of fiery words, He told me one thing: "The book is the way through."

I knew God was telling me to write a book. But I was less than willing to be a part of this particular plan. I had a book idea, but all my attempts to move forward in the publishing process had led to a dead end. Besides, a book requires coming up with sixty thousand words, and I had used up all my words for the next millennium informing God about all the ways He was letting us all down.[46]

I filed away God's singular sentence for months. To my credit, I didn't do something drastic like buy a ticket on a boat

---

[46] Be honest about your emotions with God. He can take it.

to Tarshish.[47] However, I feigned as much ignorance about what was happening as I could muster and kept myself busy with other things. I baked a lot of cookies and cakes. I played a lot of dominoes with my kids. I did 176,324 loads of laundry. I watched entire seasons of *Gilmore Girls* and *Parks and Recreation*. I joined book launch teams for other authors' books. I read dozens of books about everything *except* writing. I looked for a different word from God in ordinary things like soap bubbles[48] and my children's smiles.

I looked for a million ways to live for Jesus without writing a book because I was scared to fail.

I went to a trusted mentor and told him what God had told me. "But we all know I've failed at writing *already*. It will take a miracle for a publisher to offer me a book deal. I don't know if I can stomach the failure. If I knew it would all work out, I would do it. But I can't deal with the humiliation involved with believing God for this and then failing."

My mentor looked me square in the eyes. "That's not the way this thing works."

That's when I threw rotten eggs and tomatoes at his face while booing him.

Just kidding. That's when I burst into tears and accepted that I am one tiny person and God is very, very patient with me.

I'm not the first person to find herself in the precarious place of believing God is capable of doing the impossible. Hebrews 11 is teeming with the names and stories of people who believed God for big, big things. Despite their ambitious

---

[47] One of the hallmarks of my life is trying to avoid being swallowed by large sea creatures.

[48] This is a nod to you, Ann Voskamp. Your writing has met me in defining ways over the years. Thank you for your faithfulness to Jesus and His people.

faith, we must acknowledge that none of the people listed in Hebrews 11 was perfect. Jacob was a liar and a thief. Sarah lied about being married *and* tried to banish Hagar to her death. Moses disqualified himself from entering the promised land. Rahab was a prostitute. David was an adulterer. The dark sides of these stories tell us there is hope for all of us to make the faith hall of fame one day. I mean, Hebrews 11 names the whole nation of Israel as awesome despite the Israelites' constant complaining and that time they melted their gold into a cow to worship when the pastor was on a prayer retreat with the Almighty.

We just might be doing okay in life.

However, the encouragement gleaned from this chapter of Hebrews screeches to a halt at verse 13 (ESV): "These all died in faith, not having received the things promised, but having seen them and greeted them from afar, and having acknowledged that they were strangers and exiles on the earth."

Did you catch that? *Not one of these superheroes of the faith got their hands on what God promised.*[49]

God has always been playing the long game here on earth. He has always had a better plan including everyone in the past, you and me now, and all the people who will come after us. He wants their faith and our faith to make one completed whole, to weave us all together as He births His redemptive will for the world. Romans 8 rounds out this idea quite nicely:

> *For the creation waits with eager longing for the*
> *revealing of the sons of God. . . . For we know that the*

---

[49] Faith preachers rarely like to admit this. But it's so important that we acknowledge that Jesus is not our genie in a bottle, and faith is not a recipe for a cake you can execute the same way every time to achieve the same results. Faith is more like a casserole you make with whatever's on hand after a hard day of work. Sometimes it's delicious; other times it just feeds you enough to make it to tomorrow.

*whole creation has been groaning together in the pains
of childbirth until now. And not only the creation, but
we ourselves, who have the firstfruits of the Spirit, groan
inwardly as we wait eagerly for adoption as sons, the
redemption of our bodies. For in this hope we were saved.
Now hope that is seen is not hope. For who hopes for what
he sees? But if we hope for what we do not see, we wait
for it with patience. (vv. 19, 22–25 ESV)*

The people in Hebrews 11 had to wait beyond the days of their lives to see God's promises succeed. Romans 8 says we too are waiting along with all of creation for God's will to be birthed in the world. But I hate waiting, don't you? In our microwave, Instapot, one-click-to-buy world, we rarely have to wait for things.[50]

Except that's not true at all. We wait all the time. I have friends waiting to be healed. The world is full of people waiting to find true love that will last. Many people in my life are waiting for a baby to be born. We wait for job promotions, for our kids to figure out long division, and for the day we (hopefully) will have enough money saved to retire.

Life is full of waiting, it seems. Most of us only want to wait if we're guaranteed success. In America, success appears to be considered an inherent right for all people who patiently put in the hard work, do the right thing, and trust God will come through for them.

And yet, Jesus was, by all worldly standards, a big old failure.

---

[50] I don't have an Instapot yet, and I'm still kind of perplexed by an appliance that can cook a whole roast while I brush my teeth. What strange magic is in that pot? I bet Christians in the '80s who didn't trust Disney movies wouldn't have used one. But if you want to send one to me, I'll happily make a delicious stew in the five minutes I have between baseball practice pickup and ballet drop-off. #momwin

Jesus was poor, a child conceived out of wedlock who had a few years of massive popularity as an unofficial teacher and then was arrested and put to death. When defining success, we don't usually include capital punishment on the list of achievements one should aspire to attain. Jesus allowed Himself to be led away to suffer. He was shamed and taunted because He had spoken God's truth about how He was the Son of God. But then He withheld His power and refused to defend Himself. I wonder what His friends felt for the three days He was buried in that grave. His disciples had left their families and homes to follow Him, and then He died, and it seemed they were no closer to redemption than before they met Him.

Two thousand years later, we have the spoiler of all spoilers about the crucifixion. We know that Jesus won the ultimate victory on the cross. We know He was resurrected. But I bet the disciples had their own list of questions about injustice and all the ways Jesus had let them down on the Saturday morning after the crucifixion.

Only Mary Magdalene and some other women faithfully arrived at the tomb to do what they knew their faith and relationship with Jesus required. Willing to look failure in the face, they would take care of the body of their Lord, even though He had left them all alone.

Showing up is often the first step toward coming face-to-face with God's surprising redemptive plan. Those of us who show up and fail are in good company, what with Jesus and all those heroes in Hebrews 11 right there along with us. #failuresinfaith

No doubt you've heard Norman Vincent Peale quoted often: "Shoot for the moon. Even if you miss, you'll land among the stars." But there have been times I have shot for the moon, failed to reach my goal, and ended up stranded in empty space with no idea how to get back home.

Which reminds me of Apollo 13.

SUCCESSFUL FAILED MOON LANDINGS

Human beings are a little moon-obsessed. Every other week it seems like we hear there's going to be a supermoon, or a wolf blood moon, or a half eclipse of a harvest moon with minor moon in reverse, so set your alarms, people! This glowing orb of rock in the sky leaves us awestruck.

We all know what happens when the moon hits your eye like a big pizza pie. We know that a cow can jump over the moon in a world where dishes and spoons run away together. What woman hasn't swooned a little when George offers to lasso the moon for Mary in *It's a Wonderful Life*? In *An American Tail*, Fievel and his sister sing about "Somewhere Out There," where someone they love is thinking about them under the same moon. An ancient Chinese poem by Zhang Jiuling, who lived from AD 675 to 740, expresses Fievel's same awe of the moon:

> *Brightening the whole of heaven,*
> *Brings to separated hearts*
> *The long thoughtfulness of night. . . .*
> *It is no darker though I blow out my candle.*
> *It is no warmer though I put on my coat.*
> *So I leave a message with the moon*
> *And turn to my bed, hoping for dreams.*[2]

The moon so captivated humanity that once people could launch rockets, we knew exactly where we wanted to go someday. The Space Race was born when the dream of moon-walking met the tense relationship between America and Russia in the late twentieth century. An entire generation of people was raised believing that whoever could get to the moon first would literally win some kind of cosmic award. They circled up around their televisions to see Neil Armstrong take "one small step for a man, one giant leap for mankind."

Shortly after Apollo 11 landed on the moon, Apollo 13 was supposed to land on the moon. It failed. I know this not because I am a master of twentieth-century space trivia, but because I watched the Hollywood movie about it.[51]

NASA deemed the Apollo 13 mission a "successful failure" because of all they learned from figuring out how to rescue the crew and bring them home.

I like the ring of that phrase, "a successful failure"; it sort of sums up everyone I know in one way or another. We all lean a little more toward "successful" or "failure" by degrees. I know which way I tend to drift.

PRIDE AND (SELF-)PREJUDICE

I've never been a naturally confident person. For years, as I read the Proverbs, I skimmed past the verses about pride because a person as insecure as I was needn't worry about being prideful. I never thought I was the best or the greatest or that I deserved any grand glory. In fact, I suspected the worst might happen someday, that everyone would discover I was really made of nothing special at all.

I equated this low-level insecurity with humility, which

---

[51] Are you beginning to wonder if I only watch Tom Hanks movies? I promise I'm not that weird. But the man has been in some really amazing movies. (Let's maybe ignore *Joe versus the Volcano*, though, okay?)

was terribly convenient since humility is a hallmark of godliness. But as with our brother Cain, sin was lurking at my door, a wolf in sheep's clothing. My incorrect definition of insecurity had opened the door and invited the wolf to tea.

Then one day, I heard a sermon[3] by Tim Keller about pride.[52] Keller unraveled my carefully knit shield of self-righteousness by informing me that pride and insecurity are fruits of the same root problem: self-focus. He ripped open my insecurity and showed me that all my self-defeating fear of failure was not humility or meekness but a festering mound of sin.

My pity parties were never as much fun after that.

In Keller's book *The Freedom of Self-Forgetfulness*, he says that to end our self-focus, we must be Gospel-humble people. He points to C. S. Lewis, who says in *Mere Christianity* that pride is the central sin we all must face, and that truly humble people would not be self-obsessed in either a self-defeating view of themselves or an exaggerated self-congratulatory view of themselves. Keller posited that we can test whether or not we are self-obsessed by evaluating our response to criticism, because criticism can only wound those who prize what other people think.[4]

As you might guess, I failed the test. I had to face the truth that insecurity told me it would be better never to try than to try to do something and risk being seen as someone who doesn't have what it takes to succeed.

When I added all this up, I realized I didn't know much about success or failure at all. Hebrews 11 proves that heroes

---

[52] It seems safe to listen to sermons on topics you feel don't apply to you. Invariably, though, you find out you should be in sackcloth and ashes because great is your sin. This is all further proof Jesus be juking us all day around here.

of faith don't succeed all the time; Romans 8 says that the spiritual life is full of waiting. Apollo 13 made me consider how some failures are successes, and being overly aware of my own self had opened the door for sinful self-love or self-hate.

I was confused by all this information. One question begged to be answered in my soul: What does success really look like in the Christian faith?

Well, for Christian women, there is no doubt where we can look for the most successful woman in the Bible.

Hello, Proverbs 31.

MY RAPPER NAME IS LI'L P31

It's been a few years since I've heard a decent Proverbs 31 sermon. For a while there, in the 1990s, we Christian gals all sat in our denim overalls and Steve Madden slides and dreamed of the day some man would stand up and say, "Many women have done excellently, but you surpass them all" (v. 29 ESV).

We had a lot of work to do to get there, though, and every time this passage was preached to us, single women left feeling a little less-than, and married women went away feeling overwhelmed with all they should be doing to earn the approval of their husbands.[53]

I have been told that the noble wife in Proverbs 31 can be considered the personification of wisdom. However, that was never the way it was preached to us. It was always held up as a gold standard—that if we were women who feared the Lord, we would produce all sorts of fruitful blessings for our families and communities.

Part of the problem we faced was that we read Proverbs 31

---

[53] And also God's approval, but this isn't a therapy session, so let's leave that one alone for the time being.

through the lens of our modern brokenness.[54] Many cultural and sociological factors have resulted in women feeling like they are responsible for the care of everyone, and that their identity is wrapped up in their ability to marry, have children, and build a productive, profitable, *happy* home. But we have also been told that, like Barbie,[55] we can become anything we set our minds on. We just need to *go for it*. (And make sure everyone is okay while we pursue our dreams.)

I know what you're thinking, my few male readers. *Proverbs 31? How does that apply to me, except to give me a template for how to find the perfect woman?* I bet you've never even heard this passage preached. Because it's clearly *for the ladies*.

Except Proverbs 31 is wisdom that was given to a man, written down by a man, in a book originally read by men. It's strange, the way we've divided up the Bible in this way, making some parts for men and others for women. However, women are well-accustomed to taking passages written about men and applying the virtues taught in them to their own feminine lives. How many women have rejoiced at being lumped in with the sons of God being revealed in God's kingdom in Romans 8? We have learned to consider the word *man* as including us in many instances. Possibly, there is something here in Proverbs 31's virtuous woman for all the guys reading this book after all.

What should we do with the most awesome woman in the Bible who succeeded in every endeavor she undertook? What is here in this passage about wisdom that can reveal in greater

---

[54] The other part of the problem was the massive appeal of moralism. But I may have to write another book altogether about all the ways moralistic teaching robs us of the sweetest parts of the Gospel.

[55] Yes, I'm picking on Barbie. She's so unrealistic! Stop trying to look like her with fake faces, you guys. Really, the contouring makeup tutorials and four-inch-long eyelashes have gotten out of hand.

measure the Holy Guacamole nature of our deep belovedness to God?

If we come to Proverbs 31 reading it as a literal description of the GWOAT (greatest wife of all time), let's at least admit our P31 wife is fictitious. This is an oracle that King Lemuel's mother told him, and mothers throughout the ages have wanted more for their sons than their sons ever deserved.

A closer look at the opening words of Proverbs 31 reveals that this same mother required a great deal of her son, as well.

> *What are you doing, my son? What are you doing, son of my womb? What are you doing, son of my vows? Do not give your strength to women, your ways to those who destroy kings. It is not for kings, O Lemuel, it is not for kings to drink wine, or for rulers to take strong drink, lest they drink and forget what has been decreed and pervert the rights of all the afflicted. Give strong drink to the one who is perishing, and wine to those in bitter distress; let them drink and forget their poverty and remember their misery no more. Open your mouth for the mute, for the rights of all who are destitute. Open your mouth, judge righteously, defend the rights of the poor and needy. (vv. 2–9 ESV)*

You could look at this passage as a mother's desperate hope that her son will lead with wisdom, nobly serving his people, and choose a wife who will do everything her husband and her nation will need her to do so all can thrive.

My own mama's heart wonders if she was worried about what foolish choices could cost him. I'm afraid I've been there a few too many times with my own sons.

Recently, I was alone in the car with one of my sons, and I brought up a sore subject. I asked him to tell me how he was doing with a particular problem in his life. There had been many late-night chats about this specific situation. We had given him books to read. We had encouraged him to seek the counsel of his youth pastor. We had offered our own advice. We had prayed long and hard for him to reconcile the forces that seemed to be swirling in his life.

I longed to see him come out of the fight a blazing success. I would have done anything to ensure a happy ending for him. But I was a powerless bystander, so I kept cheering for him and watching him give it all he had. Then his circumstances went a little upside down, and nothing worked out like he had hoped it would.

So there in the car, I asked him how he was doing with the failure. I also asked him to tell me what we had done as parents that was helpful and what we had done that we shouldn't do the next time.

My son's feedback proved that I was a good mom, but not a perfect P31-wise mom. God had come through by showing my son that his success or failure did not define him. And God had come through for me by proving that while God Himself is a far superior parent than I, my love and involvement are of paramount importance in my son's life.

Maybe the point of Proverbs 31 is that none of us can ever really measure up to this high standard; not one normal human being has ever fully personified wisdom. Perhaps the best we can shoot for is not the moon, but the heart of God, whose mercy triumphs over judgment. And as we seek to walk in the fear of God, it's vital that we find spouses and friends whose hearts are aimed similarly, and that we learn to honor them in our relationships.

To be sure, our triune God, who dwells in a perfect community of love, never meant for success to be achieved all on our own. We're going to need some help to attain it.

THESE ARE NOT YOUR PEOPLE

You don't have to be an excellent wife to succeed in life. Nor do you have to be a perfect leader who obeys all his mother's wisdom.[56] In fact, Romans 8 offers us all something King Lemuel's mother never could have conceived possible. It provides us with permission to have weaknesses and the opportunity to be conformed to the image of God's Son, no matter who our earthly parents may be:

> *The Spirit helps us in our weakness. For we do not know what to pray for as we ought, but the Spirit himself intercedes for us with groanings too deep for words. And he who searches hearts knows what is the mind of the Spirit because the Spirit intercedes for the saints according to the will of God. And we know that for those who love God all things work together for good, for those who are called according to his purpose. For those whom he foreknew he also predestined to be conformed to the image of his Son, in order that he might be the firstborn among many brothers. And those whom he predestined he also called, and those whom he called he also justified, and those whom he justified he also glorified. (Romans 8:26–30 ESV)*

---

[56] Unless you are my son, in which case, please ignore my book and just do what I say. Wait, that is counterintuitive somehow. And possibly hypocritical. Okay, fine, I surrender, Jesus. Dear Jude, Jack, and Jase, love and obey Jesus, and humor your weird mom when she makes no sense whatsoever.

The Gospel means that despite everything old King Lemmy's mom said we need to do to be worthy of honor, God has taken full responsibility for our success as God's children. Jesus handed us His sinlessness and then gave us the Holy Spirit to help us when we're weak. Proverbs 31 is all about how wisdom can make a man or a woman awesome. Romans 8 is all about what God never stops doing to make us like Him. Notice most of the verbs in this passage (helps, searches, intercedes, foreknew, predestined, called, justified, glorified) have God as the subject, and we are the recipients of the action.

This means God's people can rest in all the work He's already done and receive an inheritance as His heirs. For some of us, the sit-back-and-don't-sweat-trying-to-be-awesome life comes more naturally than it does for others. My family is a mixture of Dude Perfect achievers and Party On, Wayne! chillaxers. It makes for an entertaining life.

For example, when our kids were tiny, we signed them up for sports at the local YMCA. One of my sons was naturally competitive from the very beginning. He scored eight goals in his first soccer game, and all the other four-year-olds on the field looked like cones as he dribbled around them like a miniature blond Messi. The coach pulled him out at the half because she hoped that if he wasn't on the field, the other kids would at least get to touch the ball.[57]

Our other son completely refused to go on the field. He could play soccer. He liked playing at home. But in front of all those other people, he was as stubborn as could be. We ended up using gummy worms to bribe him into playing. This poor

---

[57] This coach robbed my son of the chance to score sixteen goals in one game. But I was kind of glad she pulled him. As much as I loved watching him exult in every goal, it was getting a tad obnoxious and embarrassing to the other parents.

negotiating tactic was totally worth the sight of his cute little three-year-old legs running up and down the field *away from the ball*. I have zero regrets.

The YMCA was good to us for many years after that. Sure, they didn't *technically* keep score, but it was inexpensive and a positive environment, and we all knew when we had won or lost.[58] Then one year during baseball, we hit a snag in our YMCA experience. Our team was in the field, and our opponent was batting. One of our players fielded the ball and threw it to the player at second base, who successfully tagged the runner for the out. It was a miracle play for eight-year-old boys. But the runner stayed on the base instead of returning to the dugout. Morgan was coaching our team, and he pointed out to the umpire that the runner was still standing on second base.

The other coach shrugged and said, "Yeah, but let's just let him run the bases anyway."

The umpire agreed.

Flummoxed. That's the only word that can describe Morgan's expression when this player was allowed to stay on base after being called out by the umpire. From his perspective, at this point, the boys weren't learning how to play the game of baseball at all. He was lost in the Ecclesiastes of baseball leagues—every hit and out was meaningless.

I looked at Morgan after the game and said, "These are not our people."

You see, we are what you could call a competitive couple. What's the point of playing if you can't win? Why practice

---

[58] Dear YMCA, All the kids and parents still keep score. We have all found a loophole in your system—we are still cognizant humans who can add. Just go ahead and count the points up officially. Sincerely, All the Moms of the Kids Who Scored

batting if a triple is the same as a kid who runs the bases backward, and they let him stay on third because it's just for the fun of playing?

Romans 8, though, flexes its grace muscle in the face of my self-righteous need to prove my worth by earning a trophy. Not to burst your achiever bubble or anything, but it may be more biblical than we realize for the YMCA to be handing out trophies to everyone who shows up to play. God has always had a trophy waiting for us. Jesus just came to seal the deal and pass it out.

Somehow we must reconcile the way our spiritual development requires we practice and develop the talents God has given us[59] with the way grace allows us space to fail and be rescued by God. Compared to our omniscient, omnipotent God, we all have the talent of an eight-year-old boy who doesn't deserve to be on second base. Except after the game, we find out that God wrote us down in the book as achieving a walk-off home run.[60]

God delights in our successes the same way I delighted in my four-year-old's exuberant eight goals. Likewise, God delights in our failures the same way I delighted in my other son's aversion to the ball. I was just so happy to see him out on the field. I pray that if you've never been cherished for all the ways you excel *and* all the ways you are obnoxiously missing the point, you will find people who will do that for you. That's how God loves you, and people like that exist, I promise.

I told you at the beginning of this chapter that when God told me the book was the way through, I looked for a million

---

[59] There's a whole parable about this, of course (Matthew 25:14–30; Luke 19:11–27). And it clearly tells us God cares deeply about how we steward what He's given us.

[60] If you don't know what a walk-off home run is, it's okay. Just know it's a really big deal.

ways to live for Jesus without writing a book because I was scared to fail. I know now that was ridiculous. Living in obedience to Jesus is the very definition of success. If God was asking me to write a book, then anything else I chose to do instead was sin and disobedience.

This book *was* the way through for me. It is a successful failure that has helped me find the way home to God. I don't know if it will sell ten copies or a hundred thousand copies. Like all the big things we try to do in our lives, this book could wind up being the first of many big things I do, or the thing I did that everyone eventually forgets. But neither outcome will change God's love for me, or all He plans to do in my life.

Just like "Houston," we all have many problems. We have successes and failures. But if you count up all our problems, being separated from God's love is never going to be one of them, and His love will never fail us.

CHAPTER 10

COMPARISON AND THE RICH UNCLE

How Keeping Score Can't Save You

THERE HAVE BEEN VERY FEW MOMENTS IN MY LIFE
WHERE I HAVE ACTUALLY WISHED I HAD ONE OF THOSE
ENORMOUS CRÈME PIES YOU CAN JUST SMASH IN
SOMEBODY'S FACE. BUT THIS IS DEFINITELY ONE OF THEM.
LORELAI GILMORE, *GILMORE GIRLS*

A few years ago, I visited a friend's house for the first time. From the moment I entered, I was bombarded with exquisite beauty. Everywhere I looked I saw things I longed to own and have. I don't mean that I was seeing these things for the first time and thought they looked nice. I mean I had a list of dream purchases in my life, and they were all somehow in this particular house. It was as if every Pinterest board I had created had miraculously manifested in one location. My eyes moved from the flooring she had chosen to the art on the walls to the lights hanging from the ceiling and finally to God, who had decided to allow me to walk naively into this den of jealous temptation. The death of my contentedness was complete. This new friend of mine lived in a dream world that proved I was totally basic and rendered me physically sick with envy.

Despite the nausea my sinful heart was causing, when she offered me some tea and pulled out the chips and salsa, I was like, "I'mfinenobigdealwhat'supwithyou."

I excused myself to the most perfect powder room ever so I

could scrape myself off the immaculate parquet floors and ask Jesus to help me survive the rest of the visit.

On my way to the bathroom, I texted my husband and told him I might not make it out of this perfect house alive. I had accepted that my jealousy would probably cause my heart to explode at some point during this visit, so I asked him to please take care of the children and our Ikea furniture sitting on our 1990s cream tile floors.

Morgan texted back something like, "So sorry. Must be hard."

I pretended to believe he meant that in a supportive way.

The Holy Spirit met me there in my dream bathroom. He offered me a new version of the tenth commandment:

"Let her have her things."

Those words stopped me dead in my tracks. They were so simple and yet so freeing.

Let her have her things. There was really no reason not to. The truth, if you pressed me to be rational and honest, was that I knew she had a stack of troubles as high as anyone else's. I cognitively recognized her life was far from perfect. And for goodness' sake, this was a person I loved—like, really and truly loved, and yet I'd forgotten that when I was blinded by the material blessings in her life.

The secret sauce in my sin was that her blessings lined up solidly with all the things I wished I could have someday. What were the odds this person would have the exact chandelier from an obscure online shop above her kitchen table that I had wanted for two years? Her abundance exposed what felt like scarcity in my life. I involuntarily (and wrongly) deduced that since she owned everything I had always wanted, I would never own any of it. My covetous heart was trapped in the wilderness of comparison.

I'm pretty sure every human on the planet is vulnerable to the trap of comparison since God made sure to warn us about it in the Ten Commandments. It's as if He was letting us know that we would save ourselves all sorts of pain if we could set our wills on refusing to want what belongs to someone else.

But why does God care so much that we let other people have their things? Breaking the other commandments seems so much more dangerous. It's easy to see how murder, lying, stealing, and adultery can cause enormous problems in the world. But my friend never knew how envious and dark my heart was that day. Envy and comparison are internal and so easy to hide. I mean, really, besides it making me emotionally unstable during a hangout, what was so bad about comparing my stuff with my friend's stuff?

WHEN MOSES DROPPED THE MIC

I realize that Jesus came and gave us a new commandment, but so much of God's heart can be understood by looking at the original commandments He gave Moses when the Israelites were hiking around looking for the promised land. God wanted them to be honest and faithful. He knew that if they could honor the Sabbath, worship only the one true God, and live lives that showed respect for other people, then they would avoid many complicated and painful consequences. Really, these commandments were God's way of saying, *"I love you."*

But that tenth commandment seems a little strange, given the circumstances the Israelites were in just then. They were wandering through the desert, homeless and hungry, and Moses came at them like, "Don't you dare covet someone else's stuff." It seems to me the Israelites were probably early adopters of the magic of tidying up and minimalism, thinking to themselves, *No problem, Moses. I don't want to carry one more thing on my back. A heavier load does not spark joy in my life.*

Of course, God was doing more than drawing a boundary around our stuff with this commandment. He was telling us not to compare our circumstances or possessions or spouses with those of our neighbors, because He knows comparison and jealousy are toxic to our souls and to our communities.

And yet every marketing company in the world has one goal: to make us want things. Marketers actually rely on us wanting all the things our neighbors have because they know the power of comparison in the human heart.[61] They know the comparison game is insanely fun to win, and that we will naturally jump in the game when the opportunity arises.

As Exhibit A, I present to you this conversation with my son after school one day:

> *Me: "How are your teeth feeling after your orthodontist appointment this morning?"*
> *Him: "My whole face is sore."*
> *Me: "Want me to take you to get some ice cream?"*
> *Him: "Yes."*
> *Me: "Okay. I'll get some for the other kids too."*
> *Him: "Can you get me a bigger ice cream than you get them since I'm the one whose teeth hurt?"*
> *Me: "Why? Will your ice cream taste better if you have more than they do?"*
> *Him (smirking): "Most definitely. Yes."*

---

[61] I realize it's shocking to think that retailers don't care about the health of your soul or your heart of gratitude, but capitalism isn't known for its ability to boost cultural morale through self-denial.

My son's honesty is unparalleled. He is entirely correct—it is delicious and decadent to be given a larger portion than other people receive. It may be immature or feel shameful to admit it, but if we leave our hearts unguarded and unchecked, we all end up there, comparing our stuff with someone else's stuff just to see who won. And we desperately want to win. Winning the comparison game pays out abundantly because it strokes our pride.

But woe to us when we lose this comparison game. We end up crying in the powder room, texting our husbands about how much we hate the tile in our own houses. If God never intervened and commanded us to let other people have their things, we might end up never going back to our friends' houses again. We would lose good friends over stupid stuff and miss out on all the ways God had planned to use those friendships to bless our lives, families, and communities.

Comparison is a hustle that never pays off, and yet the world has always been full of comparison hustlers. Take, for example, the Pharisee Jesus told us about in His parable:

> "Two men went up into the temple to pray, one a
> Pharisee and the other a tax collector. The Pharisee,
> standing by himself, prayed thus: 'God, I thank you that
> I am not like other men, extortioners, unjust, adulterers,
> or even like this tax collector. I fast twice a week; I give
> tithes of all that I get.' But the tax collector, standing far
> off, would not even lift up his eyes to heaven, but beat
> his breast, saying, 'God, be merciful to me, a sinner!' I
> tell you, this man went down to his house justified,
> rather than the other. For everyone who exalts himself
> will be humbled, but the one who humbles himself
> will be exalted." (Luke 18:10–14 ESV)

This story gets at the heart of comparison. Comparison tricks us into thinking that keeping score of who is the best will save us. But in this broken world, no matter how good we are at following the rules, no matter how charming our chandeliers or how much ice cream we get, we will lose the comparison game. A day is coming when we'll realize we've been playing solitaire this whole time without any aces in the deck.

God has never been comparing us to each other. He has never offered us justification through being the GOAT[62] because God made each of us His Holy Guacamole with great delight and purpose. Our belovedness can never compare to anyone else's anywhere in the world because being loved by God isn't a competition to win.

To break free from the pride that compels us to seek a way to save ourselves through comparison, we're going to have to burn all our scorecards.

CALL YOUR RICH UNCLE

Jealousy and envy are often described as a kind of flame. We say that people "burn with jealousy" or that someone's envy "burned" against an enemy. The pride of comparison is a kind of moat around our souls to keep the fire of jealousy contained. The only problem is, that moat of pride keeps us marooned on an island, alone with our scorecards and hope for self-salvation.

How can we set fire to our scorecards without risking a blaze of epic proportions?

---

[62] GOAT = greatest of all time. In the NBA, the player most deserving of this title is heavily debated. I think we need to design a GOAT video game and put all the favorite players against each other and let the science of Nintendo reveal a winner. It would be like a basketball reality TV show, except in a video game. Call me, video game designers of the world. We will patent it and make millions.

I offer you one glorious and powerful phrase: *eternal perspective*.

If comparison is the thief of joy, then perspective is the rich uncle who flies his private jet to our island with supplies to fill in the moat and build a bonfire with our useless scorecards. Uncle Perspective then sits by the fire and tells us about all we stand to inherit as God's heirs and how our current circumstances can't even compare to all that God has planned for us.

"Look around your lonely island," Uncle Perspective says. "You're the only thing here included in God's eternal, loving plans. You're keeping score like this is the world championship, but it's more like a scrimmage to see how much you can learn."

Uncle Perspective knows we take none of our possessions with us. In the ultimate upsizing of all time, this world of asphalt and pain will pass away, and God will usher us into a world of glory beyond the scope of our imaginations.

In fact, when we really think about it, it's ridiculous that we yearn for possessions as we do. One day, even that gorgeous wooden bookcase or giant television or trendy pair of expensive shoes will become old garbage we will pay someone to take off our hands.

Uncle Perspective will also point out that the nontangible achievements we attain in this world will pass away as well. The degrees we earn will not hang on the walls of our heavenly homes. Every ribbon and award will pale in comparison to the joy of God's presence forever. The righteous and merciful acts we carry out here on earth will not be needed when God establishes His eternal will and reigns over creation in infinite grace and truth.

We take none of the evidence of our earthly glory with us

when we pass into eternity, yet Jesus' parable of the talents tells us that how we live matters. God has given each of us talents and giftings, and He cares deeply about how we steward them. He gave us the tenth commandment to guard our lives, and there is a hidden freedom in our obedience to this command. This freedom is there while we double tap Instagram posts of people whose lives are picture perfect. It pats us on the back with compassion as we stare longingly at models whose airbrushed faces taunt our own glaring lack of dermatologist procedures and plastic surgery. It tries to cover our eyes to save us from insane covetousness when we watch home-improvement marathons in which Chip and Joanna turn house after house into dream homes on budgets that seem inconceivable.[63]

The freedom in the tenth commandment is God's permission to stop hustling and step into the full story that He's writing for us. In that story, He is the hero beyond compare, who proved we are His incomparable Holy Guacamole by gifting us His Son. Nothing we achieve or create can ever do more for us than that. But once we're done trying to have the best stuff and win the comparison game, when we burn up the scorecard, we realize we don't actually know what we're supposed to be doing anymore. How do we live our lives now that we know God's plans aren't for us to be better than everyone else, but that He does care about how we live our lives?

What does it really mean to live free from comparison?

I STILL HAVEN'T FOUND WHAT I'M LOOKING FOR

Let's try to answer that question by first asking a few more.

---

[63] Indeed, this show, in particular, begs the question: If a dream house can be had for under $200,000 in Waco, why does the whole world seem to be moving to Austin and Dallas, where a home under $300,000 is impossible to find at all? Given the rising cost of housing in other parts of Texas, I predict a mass migration soon to Wacopolis.

What does freedom sound like to you? Does it sound like opening a door that has been locked for far too long? Does it sound like closing the door on a traumatic experience and knowing you never have to open it again? Is it the sound of a violin at a wedding of two people whose love will last forever? Is it the lilt of your mother's voice as she compliments you for the first time? Or maybe freedom sounds like someone thanking you for fighting to bring more justice into their world.

I think all of those beautiful sounds are echoes of what we're really looking for in life. While comparison can be a cheap substitute for any of those songs of freedom, one day a final chorus will be sung over us that will thoroughly explain the true liberty we have in Christ and the infinite extent to which we are loved.

Jesus taught us about true freedom when He told the parable of the workers in the vineyard in Matthew 20. It's a terribly unfair story about a man who hires laborers to work for him. He hires some early in the morning, promising to pay them a certain fair wage for their efforts. As the day progresses, he goes and employs more workers at various parts of the day. He hires the final group of workers when only an hour of the workday is left. At the end of the day, he pays every worker precisely the same wage, regardless of when they began working.

The workers who labored the longest feel cheated. They plead their case to their boss, who points out that he paid them what he had promised. Then he makes the bold claim that he has every right to be as generous as he wants to be since it's his money.

Jesus ended the parable with this line: "So the last will be first, and the first last" (v. 16 ESV). I don't think we wrestle enough with what this really means for us here in a *first* world nation, where we prize *first* place winners and enjoy being the *first* to get the new gadget Apple just released. We say we want the world to be fair, but I wonder if we really understand that the kind of fairness God offers is meant to set us free from having to always come in first, have the most, and be the best.

Freedom is not the same thing as comparative fairness. Freedom looks like trusting that all of God's laws and limits, His rewards and consequences, and even His mercy and judgment add up to a fair wage guarantee available to anyone who will submit to God's authority.

The wages of sin are death, but all who faithfully obey Jesus' command to love God most of all and our neighbor as ourselves will receive exactly what God promised Abraham and all of us: the great blessing of unity as God's people. There are no more lonely islands where we covet what everyone else gets and we don't. There is no more hustling to be the best. It is finished. We are loved. We belong to God and never have to be afraid of being cut off from His love.

Relax. You'll get what God has planned for you from the beginning of time. In the meantime, let her have her things. Let him do what God made him to do. Let God be God.

To carry this truth in our broken world, maybe we need to practice receiving whatever God's hand is holding out to us today—even when it seems like less than what He promised.

HANDS THAT CAN HOLD IT ALL

One afternoon I was listening to a podcast in which author Aaron Niequist led a short liturgical practice as I drove all over town shuttling my kids to and from their activities.

"If you're driving while listening, don't do this," he said.[1]

I've always been a little rebellious, so I ignored this part of the instructions. Besides, I learned to drive in Southern California during an era when police chases became nationally televised events and traffic was a fun way to play real-life Frogger. I can drive and do almost anything, Mr. Niequist. Carry on.

I was told to sit in an attentive way, feet on the floor, hands in my lap, while taking a few deep breaths, and to pay attention to the presence of God all around me. Check. Niequist then told me to hold out my right hand and imagine it held something for which I was extremely grateful. My mind put an avocado in mine. There in my hand was the symbol of everything God has done for me: the grace that I don't deserve, the forgiveness that proves I am loved, my holiness, my hope, and my chance to write this book. I began to cry a little.

Next he instructed me to hold out my left hand. This was a little challenging, what with steering my car and all. For a minute I thought maybe Aaron Niequist had been right—this was impossible to do while driving. But I am a woman who tries to be fearless as she pursues God, so I waited thirty seconds for a red light to start this part. It was a really long red light. *More proof God loves me!*

I sat at the red light at the intersection of US Route 183 and Lakeline Boulevard and imagined I was holding the most challenging thing I face in my left hand. A little dark cloud sat there, a symbol of the fear that nags me so often, the haunting of a failure, the pain of the distance we endure on earth from true love's constant voice.

The avocado and the dark cloud. I hadn't realized these two things are with me every day of my life. I carry them always but am usually only aware of either one or the other.

On good days, I see only the avocado. But on dark days, the cloud blocks my view of that green glory completely. Comparing either my avocado or dark cloud to yours robs me of the mystery of being grateful for God's blessings while at the same time aware that there is a kind of pain here on earth that will take all our lives to be healed.

At that blessedly eternal red light, I placed both my hands over my heart. I imagined God's hand over mine, and I heard Him say the thing I always need to hear Him say: *"It's all going to be okay."*

Maybe that's what God was really telling Abraham way back when He called him to leave his home: *"Walk free. It's all going to be okay."* Maybe that's what He was saying when comparison first darkened Cain's heart against his brother: *"Be free. Sacrifice what you ought to sacrifice. It's all going to be okay."* Maybe that's what He was telling Naomi when Boaz redeemed her land: *"You are free. Your life is not as bitter as you once thought. It's all going to be okay."* Maybe the good news can best be summed in that exact statement: *"All I have done is to set you free. It's all going to be okay."*

In the quiet, private place of your connection with God, there is a promise of God's goodness toward you that will nourish you in ways nothing else will. It is a shame we are such a public people. We have forgotten, as a culture, the holiness of a tender and private exchange with someone. As we post every sweet thought we have about the friends we rely on, the children we love, the partners we cherish, and the God who intimately pursues us, we are in danger of losing the plot of Matthew 6:

> *"Beware of practicing your righteousness before other people in order to be seen by them, for then you will have*

no reward from your Father who is in heaven.

"Thus, when you give to the needy, sound no trumpet before you, as the hypocrites do in the synagogues and in the streets, that they may be praised by others. Truly, I say to you, they have received their reward. But when you give to the needy, do not let your left hand know what your right hand is doing, so that your giving may be in secret. And your Father who sees in secret will reward you.

"And when you pray. . .go into your room and shut the door and pray to your Father who is in secret. And your Father who sees in secret will reward you."

(vv. 1–6 ESV)

God offers us rewards that the world will never understand or even acknowledge. Hold out your hands. You hold in your right palm God's belovedness. In your left hand, you hold the world's estimation of you, whatever that may be. No matter how successful or prosperous you are, this earthly reward cannot compare to God's reward. Hold your earthly reward loosely. See it for what it is: a flimsy promise scribbled on paper that will burn up one day when you leave this world.

By the time my red light finally turned green and I arrived at my son's high school, I felt as though a strange weight had been lifted from my life. It was as if a burden I had been dragging around had been cut loose, and I realized, suddenly, how very *not* alone I was that day.

THE COOL OF THE DAY

I once read the transcript of an NPR report[2] about a study by psychology professor James Coan in which he monitored the brain activity of a person who was hooked up to a machine that doled out electromagnetic shocks. The person sat in a chair, and a little light would come on indicating there was a one-in-five chance a shock was on the way. When the red light came on while the person was sitting alone or holding the hand of a stranger, the danger regions of the brain lit up like crazy. But when faced with the possibility of pain while holding the hand of a good friend, the person's brain stayed completely quiet. It was as if the brain knew everything would be okay as long as that friend was there.

Connection and friendship help us endure the hard parts of life and give us peace during the pain. From a Christian perspective, this truth is highlighted by God's own declaration in Genesis 2: "It is not good that the man should be alone; I will make him a helper fit for him" (v. 18 ESV).

From the beginning, God knew people needed companionship. Our three-in-one God exists in community, and when He created us in His image, He created us to need community as well. We are designed for connection.

However, we can only see this is true *after* Eve comes into the picture. When God created the first person, He didn't call him a man. The Hebrew word for "Adam" is derived from *adamah*, which means "earth." It is a gender-neutral noun. God simply made a person in His image, and then God decided Adam shouldn't be alone. Like God Himself, this image-bearer Adam needed to live in relationship. So God used part of the person He made first to create a woman. These image-bearers are now called to rule the earth together, a beautiful reflection of the God whose love birthed all things.

But the story gets a little rough after that. Before God created Eve, He told Adam not to eat from the tree of the knowledge of good and evil, which was at the center of the garden, or he would risk death (Genesis 2:17). But, as we know all too well, Satan tricked the people made in God's image into thinking who they were and what they had wasn't enough. The serpent compared people to God and told them people came up lacking. So Eve reached for a piece of fruit to make her more than she was and offered it to Adam. They were never the same again.

But when God came to find them in the cool of the day, they were not more like God. For the first time ever, Adam and Eve realized they were vulnerable and naked. Their connection to God had given them a security that was lost when they disobeyed His command. This new knowledge made them very afraid.

Standing today in the cool of the day and in God's presence, surely we can see how, compared to God, we are quite weak and limited. While that offends our pride and desire to be powerful, it doesn't bother God one bit. He is always looking at humanity as we run about trying to be more than we were made to be and asking, *"Who told you that you were naked? Who told you that you needed to save yourselves? Who told you to compare yourself to Me or to everyone else?"*

This is why He sent His Son, and it's why He has given us a commandment to love God most of all and others more than ourselves. When a shock of pain enters our lives, we need a God who is bigger than the pain and a loyal friend's hand to hold. The new commandment Jesus gave us is less of a how-to for life and more of an invitation to live in community the same way the Father God, the Lord Jesus, and the Spirit of God live in perfect communal unity.

Comparison erodes community, but love unites us in the security of our connection with God.

We were not created to be alone, and it's not good for us to be isolated. Being Holy Guacamole means recognizing our own worth and value as well as God's deep belovedness of every other person around us. That knowledge emboldens us to burn our scorecards and look at life with an eternal perspective. It frees us to take the final plunge into God's blessing by connecting with the people who love God in our communities. Together, we can hold hands when life is painful. Cheer one another on to do hard things in faith. Drop off dinner when someone needs some care. Call them to see how they're doing. Invite them over, no matter what kind of flooring we have or how on-trend our light fixtures are.

It's true that we will carry none of our achievements or possessions with us when we enter eternity. But love is eternal, and every choice and deed done in love lights our way home to God.

Go and love people well. Let them have their things and trust that God has placed all you need in your hands. It's all going to be okay.

CHAPTER 11

IN THE LIGHT OF AN ORDINARY DAY

How Fame Can't Save You

THE FRAME OF A SOUL WAS NEVER MADE FOR FAME.
THE FRAME OF A SOUL WAS MADE TO SERVE.

ANN VOSKAMP[1]

My friend Cori was teaching elementary-aged children at church one Sunday, and she asked the students what they wanted to be when they grew up. A little boy raised his hand in that exuberant way excited children do when they either need to pee super bad or have something they *must* tell the *whole class*.

"What do you want to be, buddy?" Cori asked.

"A YouTube star!" he shouted.

The boy wasn't entirely sure what he wanted to be famous *for* on YouTube, but he would figure that out later. He had time to hone a talent for something. YouTube wasn't going anywhere anytime soon, after all.

Because I am a solid member of Gen X, I laughed when I heard this goal. But, as my kids love to tell me, people make six figures these days playing video games on YouTube.[64] And, compared with the traditional and incredibly elusive worlds

---

[64] Dear millennials and Gen Z people, we old people mean no disrespect to you, but we can't believe a grown person with a college degree can support a whole family by playing video games online for others to watch as entertainment. It's kind of like how you can't comprehend a world in which random reruns were our only hope for seeing a missed episode of our favorite show. The gap between us is great, and yet we are united in Christ. Mysteries abound.

of Hollywood/Fortune 500/gold-record fame, internet fame actually seems attainable because it's so easily accessible.

Over the past ten years or so, the internet has become a content machine, churning out more blogs, ministries, and businesses than is conceivable. It has also given us all platforms on which to share our thoughts, opinions, and ideas. Magazines used to tell us everything about the private lives of celebrities, but now we tell everyone on social media about our own private lives. Who needs the paparazzi when I can see all those selfies on Instagram? Internet fame is a renaissance of every middle school popularity contest mixed with honest conversations and funny memes to pass the time.

Maybe this phenomenon just proves what has always been true: everybody is famous somewhere.

For example, in my twenties, I was famous in a little coffee shop in Corona del Mar, California. I sold sofas in the boutique next door, and most days I got free coffee for simply walking through the door and saying hello. I tried not to let the privileges of my stardom go to my head as I sipped my lattes.

In my thirties, my fame spread far and wide through the rooms of my own home. Not to brag, but *no one* changed diapers or cleaned up vomit as well as I did back then. Haters to the left, baby. I was also famous for whipping up a mean chocolate chip cookie, and my rendition of "Amazing Grace" brought down the house at bedtime.

These days, I guess I'm sort of famous for being married to the pastor of our church— which is awfully weird, frankly. One day last year, a man I had never met before approached Morgan after the service to chat, and he mentioned he had seen me in Costco that week, shopping with all my kids.

"Did you say hi to her?" Morgan asked.

"Um, no. She seemed. . .*busy*," the man said.

I'm pretty sure he used the word *busy* as a synonym for "overwhelmed and a smidge scary to me." Bringing more than two kids into Costco generally results in a kind of temporary loss of all sense exhibited by spending $300 on granola bars, winter mittens, a Fitbit, and five pounds of fancy cheese, even though you only went to Costco to grab a lunchtime hot dog deal and a box of eight tubes of toothpaste.[65]

So when dozens of book publishers told me they would be happy to pay me to write a book once I was more famous and had a larger platform, I tried to tell them I am *already* famous for being scary in Costco. This wasn't exactly what they were looking for, though. They suggested a better platform could be built by finding ten thousand people who would sign up for my email list instead of spending my free time buying cheese in bulk.

But I am nothing if not obedient,[66] so I honed my skills in the arena of promotion. I tried to learn to use social media analytics and SEO tricks to beef up my numbers. I produced more content. I shared it like crazy. I submitted guest posts. I entered my writing in contests. I joined writer groups and communities. I commented more on other people's posts and shared mine that way. I tried to be the funniest, prettiest, truest, best version of myself I could muster. *I would be famous if being famous was necessary to be published, doggone it!*

Then I woke up one day and realized I felt dead inside. I felt alone and empty and lost in this never-ending hamster

---

[65] I don't know why anyone else ever buys these gargantuan boxes of toothpaste, but when you have lots of kids, they are the absolute best. Everyone gets their own tube, and there's at least one backup in case one goes missing. Poor dental health is not our destiny in Jesus.

[66] Actually, I'm not all that obedient.

wheel of platform building. I held in one hand the advice of all the brilliant marketing people, and in the other hand I held what I knew was true—the marketing and promotion side of this work was killing me.

I told God all about it, and He quoted a version of Mark 8:36 back to me: *"What does it profit a woman to gain the whole world yet forfeit her soul?"* I knew God was telling me that, while some people have souls that can weather the unique stresses of the marketing world, mine was not one of those souls, and I should probably look for another way to pursue my writing dream.

The sweetest comfort for my soul was that Jesus didn't seem to overtly seek fame and platform in His lifetime either, and yet the number of followers this seemingly common man has had is unprecedented throughout history. Jesus was a terrible marketer, actually. How many times did Jesus do miracles and ask people to keep it on the down low? How often did He retreat to a quiet place to pray? How many times did Jesus pull a smaller group of disciples away in order to give them a clearer explanation of the confusing things He said publicly? Again and again, we see Jesus being vaguely offensive and weakening His platform, yet somehow it all broadened His impact in the end.

Jesus was focused on doing what God had asked Him to do by being who He really was—the Messiah. He let the marketing take care of itself. I'm down with this very organic method of Yours, Jesus. After He was resurrected and returned to tie up the loose ends for His followers (Luke 24), Jesus did not shoot out a tweet to let everybody know He'd just defeated death:

@SonOfMan316: *Yo, I'm back. #tombupforgrabs*
#hatersgonnahate #lifebeatsdeath #petercomeseeme
#resurrected #SpoilerAlertRomeWillFall #messiah #checkit

Instead, Jesus met two of His followers on the road to Emmaus. God Himself, in His greatest moment of awesomeness, allowed them to remain unaware of His true fame and identity. He walked with them and explained how all the Hebrew scriptures were really about Him. Then when they invited Him to dinner, Jesus broke the bread for them and they realized who He really was. He promptly disappeared.[67]

Jesus was clearly famous. In fact, He had always been famous. It's just that no one really knew that everything was about Him. For generations, every law, every sacrifice, every thread of love had been pointing to the Messiah.

There is a biblical kind of famous, and it requires we have a correct understanding of ourselves as a Holy Guacamole kind of people. To find it, we have to loosen our grip on all the ways we seek to save ourselves with the kind of fame that is garnered through the approval and adulation of other people.

ALMOST FAMOUS

Biblical fame is all around us every day, but it rarely feels as comfortable as gaming in our sweatpants for thousands of dollars. Biblical fame costs us much more and lasts a lot longer than internet fame. Jesus told us all about it in Matthew 26 when a woman poured a priceless jar of perfume on His head. Though His disciples saw her action as wasteful, Jesus shed light on the true significance of that moment:

---

[67] I have always wondered why Jesus vanished like that, but I assume it had something to do with the ancient paparazzi.

"You will not always have me. In pouring this ointment on my body, she has done it to prepare me for burial. Truly, I say to you, wherever this gospel is proclaimed in the whole world, what she has done will also be told in memory of her." (vv. 10–13 ESV)

This story is in all four Gospels. There are some additional details in Luke, and John's account tells us the woman was Mary, Lazarus' sister. But in every rendition, Jesus says the woman will be famous forever, her action inextricably linked with the Gospel.

This is an earth-shattering revelation because it proves that we don't need an agent or a better wardrobe or the ability to hack into Fortnite to be remembered. We just have to be willing to admit publicly that we need a savior; to endure the scorn of all the powerful people as we admit our weaknesses; and to bless God by sacrificing anything He asks of us.

Why is that so hard to do? Often in this world, we're told to quench our thirst by being awesome all on our own. We're told if we're thirsty for more in life, we should stop being ashamed of our weaknesses and frailties. Image is everything. The opinions of others are either our glory or our doom. Worldly fame looks like another way to live a life that doesn't need living water at all, because we can be beautiful, powerful, and significant enough on our own.

But Jesus declared one ordinary woman a hero because of her devotion, and she became one of the most beloved people in the world. It would seem we only need one Person's approval to attain the awesomest status of all.

Are we thirsty enough for Jesus to see all the ways our ordinary days are full of opportunities to be famous for our faith?

SO TRASHY

One Thursday morning I heard the familiar rumble of the trash trucks on my street. My tiny dog ran and hid under my bed, because she lives in terror of the noise those trucks make. I ran in terror out the back door, because I realized we hadn't put the trash can out yet. I grabbed that big green barrel of grossness and wheeled it out the gate. . .only to see that the truck had already passed my house and was three houses down the street.

I moaned in agony. I was caught in the suburban equivalent of a sackcloth-and-ashes kind of moment.

We had forgotten to put the trash out the week before, so of course it was overflowing with refuse. I couldn't imagine how we would manage our lives if it wasn't emptied that day. So I ran down the middle of the street while still pulling the trash can, waving my free arm and shouting at the holy men who take away all our filthy bags of rubbish.

I had not tamed my bedhead yet. I was wearing the yoga pants I had slept in—and my fuzzy slippers. I hadn't brushed my teeth or done anything to make myself look socially acceptable. The trash guys looked at me with a strange mixture of pity and fear. They motioned for me to stop running toward them so they could back up the truck to help me. But I was almost there, so I ignored them and scurried on, dragging the giant trash can behind me.

After they dumped my trash, I walked slowly back up the street, laughing to myself. I imagined a famous person in my place. Would Meryl Streep run after the trash men in her yoga pants? Would Beyoncé risk the paparazzi catching her on film begging a few men to please, please not leave her alone with her mess?

No, Meryl and Queen Bey wouldn't, because they probably pay people to drag their trash cans out for them. Which is a shame, really. Their privilege means they may never learn what I learned as I hurdled the curb with a stinking mess behind me.

I learned that this tale of trash will last forever, but not because someone caught it on film and a million people read about it in a magazine. It won't even last forever because my daughter looked at me when I got home and said, "Mom, that was kind of embarrassing."

All of my small acts—the things I throw myself into, for better or for worse—will last forever because they come from my deep gratitude for all God has given me in life and my desire to fulfill my calling as a woman who loves Jesus by caring for His people.

On Thursdays, I have to make sure the trash goes out so my family doesn't live in filth. On Saturdays, I go to my kids' games and cheer for them so they will grow up knowing they are worth showing up for. On Sundays, Morgan leaves early to prepare for the sermon and I get the rest of us to church, one way or another, so we can commune with our Father. On Mondays, I go to Costco for food to nourish all of us, even though I look "overwhelmed and a smidge scary." On Sunday nights I help host a community group in my home, where we are all learning to love one another better every week.

Every day is ordinary and yet ripe with opportunities to be famous the way only Jesus people can be famous: for loving others in a way that shows we know who God really is and what He is really all about.

You are a chosen people, a royal priesthood, a holy nation, God's special possession, that you may declare the praises

of him who called you out of darkness into his wonderful
light. (1 Peter 2:9 NIV)

Every day we are part of a Holy Guacamole kind of royal priesthood, chosen by God to be grateful and faithful. The disciples looked at the woman anointing Jesus that day in Bethany and saw only how she could have been loving others better by using the wealth she literally dumped out to help the poor. But Jesus knew if she didn't first love Him, she would never care for others the way she was called to: from a heart transformed by love.

We don't have the strength to be who God created us to be without the power of the Gospel's message of forgiveness. We could do all sorts of great works and help a million people, but without kneeling before Jesus first, we would be doing these things for the wrong reasons—possibly to be famous, to earn the approval of others, or to make a business or brand great. Then we would be like so many people throughout history who have sought fame and recognition only to end up in a heap of forgotten stories.

If you don't believe most fame is incredibly short-lived, go ask five teenagers if they can name a song from your favorite band in high school. Ask your friends if they can name more than one actor their parents watched on television as kids. See if anyone under fifteen knows answers to trivia like what "Howdy Doody time" is, where jazz really started, why the lady at the end of *Romper Room* held up a mirror, what Michael Jackson's first hit was, or which president sent the first man to the moon.

Then brace yourself to feel very, very weird when you realize that what seems like important and famous knowledge to you is obscure and unimportant to other people.

James 2 teaches us that our faith is lifeless and dead if unaccompanied by works. The letter I wrote to my main crush Ricky Schroder back in the *Silver Spoons* days is long forgotten by everyone involved, because no faith was involved in that act. Even in my naive youth I knew he'd never read it and that he wouldn't care all that much about an eight-year-old girl's life. But one woman united her faith in Jesus as the Messiah with the act of pouring out all her wealth on Him to prepare Him for His burial, and she has been talked about for thousands of years now.

What are we doing that will last beyond our lifetimes? How are our lives connected to God's kingdom plan to set people free from their sins and make them a part of His holy priesthood, called to love God most of all and others more than themselves?

BEYOND ORDINARY

I have long suspected that our deep longing to be famous is linked with the true story of who humans were created to be in the beginning. Fame is a false attempt to regain the connection we once had with God before sin separated us from Him. We long for eternal significance, because we actually aren't meant to be overlooked or forgettable. But only God can offer us this.

Significance is a unique narrative in the story of God's people. Our great significance is what drew Christ to earth as a man, to live and love and even die so that we would not be separated from God any longer. In Luke 15:7 Jesus said that all of heaven rejoices over one sinner who has turned from his sin. Repentance itself is an acknowledgment of how significant our lives actually are in the universe. If our lives didn't matter, God wouldn't care who we hurt with our choices or what we are wasting when we live selfish lives and refuse to seek justice for the weak, offer food to the hungry, or fight to free the oppressed.

Therefore, unrepented sin is evidence that we have forgotten how significant we are to God. Our free will allows us the power of choice, but when we forget we are immortal beings, we lose our grasp on how beloved we are to God, and we choose poorly. We devalue people around us because we forget they are as valuable and immortal and beloved as we are. We forget we are God's ambassadors on earth, His holy priesthood, His set-apart Holy Guacamole people who bear His image. Forgetfulness is how people who were made in the image of God become victims or victimizers, users or abusers, and lonely and isolated in sin.

A famous, eternal story of good news is being told all over the earth. You are a famous part of God's story because He chose to die so you could live forever with Him. Will you offer God what is most valuable to you? Can you hand Him your reputation, your time, your words, your kindness, your prayers, your money, your food, your compassion, your career, your empathy, your effort, your love, your dreams, and your comfort?

What happens once we pour the jar of our lives out all over Jesus? Ideologically it's fantastic to know we're significant to God, but how does that impact our daily lives, in which we wake up every day and get dressed, do the laundry, pay our bills? We don't want to be like Peter in Matthew 17 and get all weird. If you recall, Peter followed Jesus up a mountain along with James and John and insisted they never leave when Jesus started glowing and chatting it up with Moses and Elijah. Peter was like an ancient superfan: "Look! All the famous people are here! I want to stay here and never leave! I'll build you guys some tents. James, make some swag bags! Let's have an after-party that never ends!"

Oh Peter, *you are our people*. We'd all like to just bask in the glory that we are God's favorites and never have to go back to our ordinary lives too. But right after Peter announced his construction plans, God's voice boomed from heaven and told him to listen to Jesus.

And then Peter, James, and John all fell down and hid their faces until Jesus looked ordinary again. Here on earth, the extraordinary is often hidden in the ordinary. I learned that way back in college when my job once required I swim in Loni Anderson's pool.

LA LA LAND DREAMS

When I was in college at UCLA, I needed a weekend job. Like most students, I lacked money in a major way. This was way back in the 1990s, long before the internet made finding a job so overwhelmingly uncomplicated. We had to physically hoof it from place to place and fill out actual paper applications. We also had a section in the newspaper called "the classifieds" that announced job openings.[68] I found an ad requesting a weekend nanny in the Valley and called the number listed.[69] I met the mom and one of the daughters in a deli off Ventura Boulevard in Studio City. We all got along really great. The mom hired me right there and asked me to start that Saturday.

---

[68] "Newspapers" were ancient twentieth-century media outlets in which the local and national news was printed on large pieces of paper and distributed by little boys on bicycles in the early hours of the morning.

[69] Calling a number was how people used to contact each other in the late twentieth century on telephones that used actual phone lines. It was similar to voice texting, except you spoke with the other person live. It was a lot like FaceTiming but had no video available and required no WiFi whatsoever. Can you even imagine?

I really had no idea who I had agreed to work for at the time. I was twenty-one years old and didn't even consider it might be helpful to know who was hiring me.[70] I just thought, *Huzzah! I have a job.* I made plans to be there Saturday morning.

That first Saturday would be the first of many times over the next few years that I took the beautiful Beverly Drive from Beverly Hills to the San Fernando Valley, up and over Coldwater Canyon. I pulled up to the large wooden gate at the house and pressed the call button.

"Hello?"

"Um, hi, this is Carrie, the new nanny?"

"Oh! Okay! Come on in."

The wooden gate slid open, and greeting me as I entered the property was a larger-than-life statue of Erik from *The Phantom of the Opera*. The house itself looked more like a storybook cottage that had been magically turned into a mansion. There in Toluca Lake, one of the most elite parts of Los Angeles, I got out of my car and looked around at what had to be several acres of gorgeous property. Nothing was really as it seemed. The koi pond looked like a wishing well, the swimming pool looked like a hidden lagoon, the playhouse had running water and nicer furniture than my apartment.

By the time I saw the *four golden Oscars* above the mantel in the study, I knew for sure I was working for very famous people.

These famous people were lovely and so normal. Ordinary, even. Of course, they had a gardening crew and full-time housekeeper and a historical suit of armor on display. But I

---

[70] In hindsight, I realize I could have ended up an unsolved mystery here. Let's not linger on how naive I was back then, though. It's way too scary.

spent my time there jumping rope on the deck with the girls and helping them with their math homework. We swam in the pool and read books and almost never watched television. I took them on playdates to the homes of soap opera producers and, yes, once I ended up playing sharks and minnows with all the kids at Lonnie's house. When the Oscars rolled around, the girls and I watched as their parents rolled away in their rented limo. Then we played hair salon, which meant they put my hair in eighteen ponytails with a different bow on each one. We watched the Academy Awards on the sofa with big bowls of popcorn and played a game called "Will your dad win an Oscar this year?" Then I put them to bed and dozed on the couch until the after-parties ended.

Every once in a while, strange parts of Hollywood life popped up in the quotidian space of these people's lives. One day the girls and I were rollerblading when we saw Bob Hope drive by in his golf cart, and he waved at us, which felt quite historic somehow. But mostly, life was ordinary there in Toluca Lake. After a year or so, I became the everyday nanny, and life was lovely and normal, even if a masked Erik did wave hello to me every day I went to work.

I often think back to those years and find it astounding that I didn't realize then how unusual it was to be cocooned in this hidden place of ordinary life. But I realize now the spiritual life in God is both ordinary and extraordinary in the same way. We are forever arriving in new places of God's kingdom, naive about what they will be like and yet also dazzled by the first glimpse of glory when it arrives. Then the longer we exist in these new places, the more ordinary they become. We get comfortable with the eccentricities and peculiarities of the Holy Spirit; we come to anticipate the miraculous parts of spiritual life with Jesus as commonplace, even though they once seemed mysterious to us.

Let me take this moment to remind you: God is not ordinary. He is the most famous being in existence. He is the most powerful force we will ever encounter. His beauty and perfection are unparalleled. He is glorious and terrifyingly mighty.

God is certainly not ordinary. But He is humble.

It is important we don't confuse these two words. While I nannied my way through college, very "ordinary" parents showed me that humility looked like setting an Oscar on the mantel and then returning wholeheartedly to mommy-daddy duty.

On a much grander scale, our extraordinary God has set His miracles on the mantel for us to see and called us over to the sofa so He can be the Father to us we long for most of all.

Don't miss your chance to sit with God because you're too busy trying to be famous in a world that will one day pass away. The humility of God has made us more significant than we often grasp. God has written a script with a part created just for you. No one else can play your role, which means you have nothing to prove or to fear. Just listen to the Son of God and faithfully pour out your life as you love all the people He created in His image.

When I graduated from college and quit my nanny job, my boss asked me if I had a friend who would love her kids and take care of them just like I had. I gave her a few names, but I had to tell her I was pretty sure no one would ever love the girls like I did. I spent all those years serving that family, drinking living water and watering a seed that would one day grow into a Holy Guacamole avocado tree in my soul. God taught me in that cottage mansion that people are not valuable because they're in magazines or because they have millions of fans. People are valuable because they are irreplaceable and worthy of love.

Who needs to be internet famous when we have a God like ours? Not me, that's for sure.

CHAPTER 12

ALL WE DO IS WIN

How Jesus Has Already Saved Us

SOMETIMES THE WINNER IS THE LOSER. . .
AND THE LOSER IS THE WINNER.
ME TO MY COMPETITIVE HUSBAND IN 2003,
WHEN HE WORKED REALLY HARD TO GET A MINISTRY
ASSIGNMENT NO ONE ELSE WANTED

I believe people are really made up of stories.

If I ask you who you are, you may have a hard time putting your whole identity into words. You might try, by telling me your age, nationality, marital status, or what you do to earn your livelihood. But these details about your life wouldn't reveal who you are.

But if I asked you to tell me about your life, you would probably tell me a story about growing up in the city or town you grew up in; a story about your parents and siblings, the tragedies or opportune moments that were turning points for you, or the time you made a choice that changed everything. You would probably even tell me stories about other people as you tried to explain your own life, sharing who influenced and shaped the person you have become.

Once I heard your stories, I would know who you are in ways that titles, degrees, and affiliations could never reveal. For example, if I told you I wrote much of this book wearing my grandfather's old cardigan because feeling the soft yarn against my skin is like a deep exhale, you might guess that I am a bit of a romantic. If I explained further that this old blue sweater reminds me that even before I was a writer, I was loved, then you might deduce truths about me that I wouldn't know how to tell you any other way.

I am made of stories. Many of them are in this book. Most of them aren't. In fact, plenty of my stories haven't happened yet. Even so, I know what they are about and how they will end.

I know because I have the Bible to remind me that every story that ever was is really about one particular Person. The Bible is one long book of stories about many, many people, written over thousands of years. All these stories are really about Jesus. He is also called the Word in John 1, and we're told the Word was before all things and made all things. This passage in John and all the parables Jesus used to teach His disciples prove God is keen to use His story to shape and light the world.

For generations, Christians have shared their stories of faith and redemption to encourage one another, calling these stories their testimonies. In Revelation 12, we are taught that when good and evil clash in one final battle, God's people will overcome and defeat their enemy through the blood of the Lamb and the word of our testimony.

His Story + Our Story = Victory.

Story is a strong game plan for winning in life. We win, in part, through owning and declaring Jesus' story and our own. I believe all of this, and yet I am also often perplexed by how many of my stories feel more like losses than wins. There seem to be more tragic stories in life than happily-ever-afters. Many days, I feel more like I am losing something than like I am an undefeatable champion.

I suppose this is because as long as we live here on earth, we are still in the middle part of our stories. The middle part is the bummer part. Movie trilogies prove this. I don't know why we bother to go to the second installment in a trilogy. It's always an overwhelmingly negative experience. Will Frodo be able to carry the ring all the way to Mordor? Will the Rebel Alliance defeat the Death Star or will the Empire win? Will the Avengers be able to stop Thanos now that he has the Infinity Gauntlet? Bible stories are also stories that have an awful lot of losing before the winning begins. The stories of Abraham and Sarah, Esther, Ruth and Naomi, David, the prodigal son and his older brother, and the Samaritan woman all fit in our category of significant losses that lead up to greater eternal victories only because of the hope of redemption.

To be brave enough to make it through the messy middle to our happily-ever-after ending, we need a better story about the kind of winning that swallows up all the losing we face along the way. I witnessed one particular victory that I return to, time and again, when I need to believe we will all win in the end. As silly and inconsequential as it sounds, it happened on a Texas Little League field.

Y'ALL NEED JESUS

A few years ago, our family arrived at the local baseball fields for an all-star championship game on a hot and sticky Texas summer night. I was wearing my favorite shirt emblazoned with the words "Y'all need Jesus." Our own personal all-star was eleven years old, and we were ready to cheer like crazy for him.

The pregame warm-up did not begin well for the fans. When we got to the field, our opponent's fans had put all their bats and bags in our home team dugout. The home team dugout was the shady one and should have been reserved for us, but now our boys would be living on the face of the sun in the away team dugout.

Baseball is a game of gentlemanly etiquette, so a group of us wandered over to politely ask the opposing group to move.

"Um, we're pretty sure you're in our dugout," we said.

"Well, the last time we played you guys, we sat in the wrong dugout," they replied.

"Yes, but that was because we had played the game before, and so we just stayed in the dugout from that game. And both dugouts were shady in that game. So there wasn't the discrepancy."

"We're already here. We aren't moving," they told us.

That was when I decided we needed to be more direct. So I stated the undeniable fact we all seemed to be hedging around.

"Can we just be honest and admit we're fighting over shade for the boys? That's what this is about, and our team has been assigned the shady dugout," I said.

The other team's parents didn't appreciate my frankness. One woman turned to her husband and said, "Look, honey, her shirt says 'Y'all need Jesus.' Don't you think *she's* the one who needs Jesus, though?"

As a matter of fact, I did need Jesus right then—very, very desperately. I needed a table-tossing Jesus to manifest Himself and either upend the other team's bench or carry me home so that I could avoid ending up on the 5:00 p.m. news with this headline under my mug shot: Pastor's Wife Arrested in Ball Field Brawl. Morgan also imagined the headline

I suppose, because he turned to all of us and said, "Let them have the shade. It's all going to be okay."

My diplomatic husband had led us on the high road, and we begrudgingly followed him. After all, it's just a game, right?[71]

But then we started *losing the game*. As the other team's runs piled up, so did the injustices. Inning after inning we watched the catcher step on our guys' hands and ankles after they slid into home. The opposing team's coach shouted at our pitchers to mess up their timing and get in their heads, predicting the pitch before they threw it: "Fastball!" "Change-up!" The other team's parents yelled terrible things about our players, including curse words. These were just kids, so *what in the world was wrong with these people?!*

Morgan had been wrong.[72] Everything was *not* okay.

I started pacing behind the bleachers, talking to God. "Lord, this isn't fair. Losing to a team like this is *the worst*. We need You to do something! Where are You, God? *You can't let the wicked prevail!*"[73]

At the start of the final inning, we were down 8–3. We miraculously scored three runs, and all we needed was two more to win. With two outs left, we were at the bottom of our lineup, so our weakest hitters would have to be spectacular.

The stress was about to make me puke.

But as I watched our batter walk up to the plate, I knew that, win or lose, our boys were heroes. They had played without lowering themselves to the level of their opponents. They

---

[71] Never in the history of kids' sports has any game ever felt like "just a game" to anyone with any competitive leaning. #facts

[72] My fickle heart loves it a tiny bit when he's wrong. It happens so rarely it's like a delicious treat.

[73] I tend to be a little dramatic when I talk to God about baseball.

had been cursed at and mocked but had come back and played beautiful baseball. They had nothing to be ashamed of.

As I mentally braced myself for the loss, I watched our weakest hitters score, and we won the impossible game. We erupted in celebration. The boys piled on top of each other. The moms jumped around like they had lost their minds. The dads were literally crying.

Then we watched in horror as the coach of the other team, who had been so rude and disrespectful all night, pulled his son out of the area under the lights shining on the field. That father stood in the darkness and screamed in his son's face. My heart broke when I heard him say he was ashamed to be his dad. Some of their players refused to shake hands. Some cursed our boys to their faces. That coach was banned the next year from the league after the umpires reported his unsportsmanlike conduct.

When Morgan tells this story, he often says that hell must look like a parent cursing his son in the darkness. I also think that heaven looks like a bunch of parents crying with joy because their kids refused to give up and then won in the end.

Ever since that time when our boys won their parents' admiration and respect long before they won the game, my favorite hashtag has been #allwedoiswin. When I say "all we do is win in Christ," I am paraphrasing 1 John 5:4–5 (MSG):

> *Every God-begotten person conquers the world's ways.*
> *The conquering power that brings the world to its knees is*
> *our faith. The person who wins out over the world's ways*
> *is simply the one who believes Jesus is the Son of God.*

The world's ways require a lot of hustle and self-salvation. The world's customs require we put ourselves first in any situation, curse anyone who gets in our way, and shame anyone who fails to live up to our expectations. When we fall and fail, it's always easier to accuse someone else of causing our failure or ruining our chance to win than it is to stand back up and look to God to be our champion.

Jesus knows this. In the Garden of Gethsemane, He felt the full weight of embracing today's pain and loss while trusting it would all be okay in the end. Now, victorious in heaven, Jesus knows it seems unjust to us that God's people are often left in a blazing hot dugout with enemies taunting them from a shadier spot. He knows what it's like to be treated like you are left out and left over. He also knows that God's story for us ends with happily ever after.

Jesus is offering us sweet refreshment in every word of His story so we can overcome the bitter days of our own. And Jesus + sweetness makes us all think of Christmas cinnamon rolls, right?

CHRISTMAS EVERY DAY

Every Christmas Eve, I bring homemade cinnamon rolls to church with me and pass them out to people. Some pans have names on them; some don't. The ones without names I give out spontaneously to whoever I run into on my way in or out of the building. One year I gave a pan to a woman I hadn't met before. She began to cry, because she was living in a shelter that year and had no money for anything special on Christmas morning for her daughter. I quickly realized that I had handed her more than breakfast—from where she stood, that pan was full of hope. This experience launched me into a sort of Christmas cinnamon roll obsession. Because of that one woman's story, every Christmas I bake extra pans for strangers who might not enjoy the abundance most of us do at the holidays.

A few years ago, I arrived at church with several of these extra pans. I had given most of them to homeless members of our congregation before the service. After we lit the candles and sang "Silent Night," I still had two pans left. Morgan had to stay to do a few things before he headed home, so I gathered up my kids, and we went on a cinnamon roll quest.

"We're looking for someone who needs a little Christmas," I said. They all nodded, and we drove slowly along the road scouring the streets for anyone we could find.

However, the temperature was dropping below freezing as I drove, and it seemed most of the homeless and poor had hidden away in their tents or shelters. I wasn't sure what we would do, and I prayed God would help us find someone. And then I saw them: a group of three men huddled together in a parking garage near an office building. We careened across traffic and pulled into the garage.

Now, it's essential for me to say that I am a city girl. I lived in Los Angeles for many years, and I know how dangerous a parking garage can be. I knew this wasn't the safest thing I had ever done. But it was Christmas, and something told me it would be okay. Just in case it wasn't, I left the motor running and told the kids to lock the doors of the car and not get out—no matter what happened. Then I said they could use my phone if they needed it for some reason. They understood the words to be a warning of sorts, but since I said them with a smile on my face, they took it in stride.

I walked toward the men and said, "Would you like some Christmas cinnamon rolls?"

That was when I realized there weren't just three men, but six. They were some of the roughest-looking street people I had encountered here in Austin, scarred and broken in body and life. Even so, they walked toward me smiling and completely relaxed.

"Merry Christmas," I said as I handed them the pans.

"Thank you," one of the men replied. He opened his arms for a hug. I didn't hesitate. Later I realized the vulnerable foolishness of this moment, but right then I only knew that I wanted them to feel the kind of friendship God intends for all of His children to experience in life and in eternity. I hugged that man and told him God loved him. Then I said goodbye. The kids let me in the car, and we drove home to our warm house, which suddenly seemed far too full of things we couldn't possibly ever deserve.

Now I only pass out cinnamon rolls during the day, when Morgan can be with us. But that night in the parking garage taught me how much we need the story of Jesus' birth to remind us that every day God is birthing love in the middle of our messy, humble stories. This world is full of bitter circumstances and failures as well as sweet privileges and victories. We have refrigerators that break down and imperfections that expose our need for salvation. We often feel like we're the leftover people who don't deserve a place on the plate of life. We long for something that can numb the pain of our cynicism and not-enoughness. We get lost in the story sometimes when sin blinds us to the victory we're assured in Christ's love and friendship.

To win in life, we must remind ourselves and each other of the great love story God has for us. Only perfect love causes fear to flee from our lives, and only love can lift the burden of shame we carry for all the times we argued for a better dugout or kept all the cinnamon rolls for ourselves. First John 4:9–12 (ESV) tells us this about love:

> *In this the love of God was made manifest among us, that God sent his only Son into the world, so that we might live through him. In this is love, not that we have loved God but that he loved us and sent his Son to be the propitiation for our sins.* **Beloved, if God so loved us, we also ought to love one another. No one has ever seen God; if we love one another, God abides in us and his love is perfected in us.** *(emphasis added)*

I wish I could say loving people comes naturally to me in all settings and situations, but cinnamon rolls aside, it often doesn't. However, I know doing so is God's mission in my life—and I want in on God's mission in my life. I also want in on His mission all around me in the world. God is writing a long, long story about His loving rescue of humankind, and I don't want to miss my cue to step in and take part in it because I'm distracted with creating the most comfortable and successful life I can for myself.

The world is full of thirsty people, and God put living water in us. Surely that means we're meant to pour it out.

THE END OF THE STORY

I am not encouraging you to adopt some kind of works-righteousness lifestyle. But I am asking you to remember the many times Jesus urged His followers to take care of other people.

Live your life accordingly.

In Matthew 25:31–46, Jesus taught us that how we serve others will matter a great deal on the day God declares His final victory:

"When the Son of Man comes in his glory, and all the angels with him, then he will sit on his glorious throne. Before him will be gathered all the nations, and he will separate people one from another as a shepherd separates the sheep from the goats. And he will place the sheep on his right, but the goats on the left. Then the King will say to those on his right, 'Come, you who are blessed by my Father, inherit the kingdom prepared for you from the foundation of the world. For I was hungry and you gave me food, I was thirsty and you gave me drink, I was a stranger and you welcomed me, I was naked and you clothed me, I was sick and you visited me, I was in prison and you came to me.' Then the righteous will answer him, saying, 'Lord, when did we see you hungry and feed you, or thirsty and give you drink? And when did we see you a stranger and welcome you, or naked and clothe you? And when did we see you sick or in prison and visit you?' And the King will answer them, 'Truly, I say to you, as you did it to one of the least of these my brothers, you did it to me.'

"Then he will say to those on his left, 'Depart from me, you cursed, into the eternal fire prepared for the devil and his angels. For I was hungry and you gave me no food, I was thirsty and you gave me no drink, I was a stranger and you did not welcome me, naked and you did not clothe me, sick and in prison and you did not visit me.' Then they also will answer, saying, 'Lord, when did we see you hungry or thirsty or a stranger or naked or sick

or in prison, and did not minister to you?' Then he will
answer them, saying, 'Truly, I say to you, as you did not
do it to one of the least of these, you did not do it to me.'
And these will go away into eternal punishment, but the
righteous into eternal life." (ESV)

I apologize for ending this book with the breezy topic of eternal judgment. Heaven and hell aren't the cheeriest of bedtime stories, and there are many different views about how all of this will play out when Christ returns. My goal is not to sort them out right here today. However, I can't talk about the final victory Jesus has planned without also talking about the darkness He has saved us from. A great deal is at stake here.

According to Jesus, if we want to be counted among the set-apart, beloved Holy Guacamole people of God, we can only move toward Him by moving toward needy people and offering them love and care. The facts are that Jesus is there with them, waiting for us to love Him by loving them. Every pan of cinnamon rolls we hand out lands straight in Jesus' hands. If we cannot find a way to love and serve others, we should ask ourselves if we really love God at all.

In our modern, Western world that celebrates tolerance and inclusion, this story Jesus tells of God's judgment seems harsh. However, that view stems from our comfortable cultural message that self-salvation is possible and the lie that everything we really need is already within us. We have tricked ourselves into subtly believing that when God sent a Messiah, there wasn't all that much we really needed to be saved from. We often frame Jesus as a really great life coach who is just there to remind us we are loved and wanted and powerful even when we feel like we aren't.

Jesus' story cannot save you if you believe He's your great encourager. Believing in a kind but nonvital Jesus is how we lose the power of Christ in our lives.

Jesus is not playing around with your story. When He taught that everything was about Him, that He is the way, the truth, and the life, He meant that you will not be able to get around Him someday to sneak into eternity with a counterfeit wristband you bought on Craigslist. It absolutely matters how we live our lives, whether we obey God's call to love and follow Him, whether we kneel before him in submission to His lordship or stand against Him, defiantly declaring that His commands seemed a little too harsh.

I hope I'm communicating that while you are a big deal to Jesus, no one is a bigger deal *than* Jesus. We have a Messiah who can tell us everything we ever did, just as He told the Samaritan woman everything she ever did. He is not a distant judge who doles out punishments and rewards from a disconnected, comfortable throne in heaven. Jesus has earned His place at the Father's right hand by suffering and dying so that He could set us free from fear and pain and defeat our selfishness and sin.

Anything we take part in that distracts us from the eternal weight of our choices in this life blocks our ability to love God most of all and others more than ourselves. Comparison turns people God loves into our enemies. Pretty things anesthetize us, so we fail to see true beauty and do the kind of justice God asks of us. Perfectionism and success lie to us and tell us to keep working hard because we are so very close to being good enough on our own. Cynicism deceives us into hardening our hearts and losing hope that God can still do miracles. Fame keeps us running after a life we will never be able to maintain, and probably don't want anyway. Doubt takes all the fun and adventure out of life. Quitting robs us of the chance to see how God can use an ordinary person like me and like you.

But Jesus has living water waiting for all who repent of their sin and worship Him as Messiah.

The hungry man on the corner is not just a man who needs a good meal. The refugee seeking asylum is not just a displaced person in need of a bed. The child in foster care is not just a kid who needs a place to belong. The man next door who is hiding in his perfect suburban life is not just a guy with a good job and a nice car. And you are not just some person living a life that doesn't really matter in the end.

You are Holy Guacamole. So are they. God is serving up His love in us and through us.

The only thing left to do is to win forever.

ACKNOWLEDGMENTS

The first problem the world ever faced happened after God made Adam and saw it wasn't good for people to be alone. It has been that way ever since, even for all of us who call ourselves introverts. God graciously gives us helpers and mentors and faithful friends who offer us courage and comfort to be who God made us to be and do what He has called us to do. I am grateful for all the people who have made my life better by not letting me quit or hide when I was afraid I didn't have what it takes.

Jesus: You are the real deal. You put up with a lot from me. You should be in charge of everything.

Morgan: It will always be you. You're my favorite winner. Please buy me tacos and kiss me like you mean it.

Jude: I love to make you laugh. Thank you for inspiring me to preach the Gospel in slang. You make me almost cool enough. (Weird flex but okay.)

Jack: I hope this book made sense. If it didn't, tell me in five years instead of today. You make me smarter. Also, can you help me set up my new phone?

Jase: No one fights to love me like you do. You make me braver and keep me safe. Let's bake a cake to celebrate.

Finley: I'm so glad God sent me a fair warrior and faithful

friend in you. You make my life more fun. Thank you for letting me write when we should have been doing math. Fourth grade is really overrated anyway. ;)

Dan and Ellen: You loved me and believed in me first. Thank you for sending me to college so I wouldn't be so dumb. Can you believe they let me write a book? I hope I've made you proud.

Brett and Melissa and Kevin and Jody: Stansted Manor was the best thing that ever happened to all of us. You have taught me what friendship really is. Let's go to Hawaii next year.

Matt and Christy: You have been faithful in every way to people and to God. You are my heroes. Everyone should have friends like you. We're ready to come back to France now.

Jessie: Thank you for believing in me and my writing when I didn't. You are an incredible agent and a blessing in my life.

Everyone at Barbour Books: My gratitude for you can't be quantified. I have never wanted to bake someone a cake as much as I want to bake one for all of you. It would be chocolate, of course, and shaped like an avocado.

David and Sandy: You taught me what grace really is, how to belong, and how not to take myself too seriously. I love you and supercalifragilisticexpialidocious.

Greg and Suzanne: You have prayed for me and believed with me a million times. Thank you for loving me so well. I'm sorry for all the times I snuck Diet Coke into your house.

Jody, Karla, Keivon, Kenny, Melissa, Mike, and Jolene: You are the greatest reader/writer friends ever. Thank you for all the encouragement. I hope you weren't lying to me to be nice.

Grady: There is no better counselor or therapist on the planet. Pretty sure Tolkien was imagining someone just like you when he created Gandalf. Thank you for everything.

Mosaic Church of Austin: You're my favorite church in the whole world. Without your love and faith, I'd never know what Holy Guacamole is. Pastors are supposed to take care of their churches, and yet you have taken such good care of us. You must really love Jesus or something.

Our Every Nation family: Morgan and I have been here since we were teenagers who wanted to change the world by loving Jesus best of all. The only thing that's really changed is our age (okay, and maybe our faces). Thank you for believing in us and letting us be a part of it all.

MAKING HOLY GUACAMOLE

HOW TO THINK, FEEL, AND ACT— CHAPTER BY CHAPTER

Some of us are great thinkers; we understand ourselves and life best when we have time to consider, ruminate on, and process all the ideas and information we encounter. Others of us feel everything first and foremost; hearts on our sleeves, guts full of intuition, we grow and learn as we face and sort through our emotions. And still others of us are people of action. We need something in our hands to achieve and act upon; we have more energy than we can contain, and we are at our best when we are making things happen.

Jesus said the most vital thing we can do is to love God with our whole heart, soul, and mind, and that we ought to love others more than we love ourselves. He taught that our inner spiritual life must be woven into the outer world we en-counter. Being God's Holy Guacamole means engaging our thoughts and feelings and actions fully as we navigate the path of life before us. Here is a short guide to help you think, feel, and act your way through the chapters of this book. You can use it on your own, in a book club, as a community group, or with a friend.

CHAPTER 1:
FROM THE WELL TO THE ICE MAKER

THINK

In chapter 1 we read, "You can never save yourself through self-improvement," and yet we know that if we are following Jesus, in our ever-changing lives, we should be growing in our Christlikeness. What is the difference between self-improvement and spiritual growth/formation? Is it possible to improve yourself and not grow in Christ? How do grace and truth work together to bring about spiritual growth in our lives?

FEEL

I wrote this in chapter 1: "Likewise, as we press into knowing Jesus and entrust Him with our imperfections and weaknesses, God's presence and power will transform us into God's holy people." How comfortable are you with facing your weaknesses and imperfections? Are there some people you feel safer sharing your vulnerabilities with than others? Can you be honest with yourself and with God about your frailties? If not, what could help you grow braver in this area?

ACT

The Samaritan woman went alone to the well as a part of her daily chores and ended up meeting Jesus. For one week, choose a daily activity, such as a morning walk, your evening dishwashing duty, or your drive home from the office, and practice being fully present and looking for God as you engage in the activity. Don't turn on music or the news while you do it. Don't multitask and make a list of all the things you need to do later. Just show up and do your job with an expectation to meet the Messiah. Listen for anywhere His voice may be hiding like it was hiding in my broken refrigerator. Who knows, He may tell you "everything about you" and you may be changed in ways you hadn't expected. I pray your whole inner life will be flooded with His living water.

CHAPTER 2:
HOLY GUACAMOLE AND LEGGINGS AS PANTS

THINK

Chapter 2 asserts, "If we're poor in spirit, we know there's nothing we can do to get our cosmic leggings to stretch adequately over our sin. God gave us the Bible as a mirror to show us the flimsiness of our attempts to save ourselves. He also gave us one another, because it's really not good for us to be alone." Friendship and biblical truth are pillars in the Christian life. Has God used scripture to help you see that you are not alone and that you can't save yourself? If so, what scriptures have helped you the most? If you have less exposure to scripture, where could you go or who could you ask to help you grow in this area? Do you currently have friends helping you feel less alone in your life? If not, what could you do to try to cultivate those kinds of friendships?

FEEL

Chapter 2 tells the story about the time I confessed to my friend that I felt like rice and beans on a plate of Tex-Mex food: no one ordered me—I just came on the plate, taking up space and not particularly wanted. This isn't an uncommon feeling, even though it is the exact opposite of what the Gospel says about us, that we are loved and that there is space for us in God. Have you ever faced a similar feeling, of being extra or unwanted? What happened that caused that feeling to be resolved? If it hasn't, what do you feel would help you accomplish this?

ACT

Jesus challenged a rich young man who wanted to inherit eternal life to sell all his possessions, give the money to the poor, and follow Him. Sometimes our lives can be full of seemingly good things that actually distract us from our ability to hear Jesus and be near to Him. Consider giving up one activity that requires both money and time for an extended amount of time (possibly a month of visits to the coffee shop or juice bar, a subscription of some kind, a membership somewhere, movie tickets, or the money you would spend shopping for luxuries like new shoes or home goods). Then purposely devote the time that activity would usually require engaging in your faith in some way (e.g., reading, studying, praying, serving) and give the money you save to an organization that cares for the poor.

CHAPTER 3:
SIT DOWN, DEBORAH

THINK

Often, in some parts of America and in some churches, women have been encouraged to serve in behind-the-scenes roles and discouraged from leadership positions that would involve more visible, up-front teaching and leading. Has that been your experience? What were the available leadership positions for women in your church, community, and family growing up? How do you think that formed you? How has your view of women in leadership changed over the years?

FEEL

When faced with potential conflict, do you tend to move into the conflict to resolve it or move away from the conflict to avoid it? What emotions trigger either your aggressive engagement or your avoidant retreat? We see Jesus react in both ways in the Gospels. Read Luke 5:12–16; John 10:22–42; and John 18:1–11. What do you think motivated Jesus' retreat or engagement in each of these stories? What can your soul learn from Him in this area of your life?

ACT

For at least seven days in a row, set aside twenty minutes each day to sit in silence. Set a timer on your phone and choose a word (*Jesus, faith, hope, quiet, peace,* etc.) to use as a mental focal point that can clear your mind when other thoughts enter (and they will!). When thoughts about your plans for the day, the tasks you need to accomplish, and the people you love enter your mind during the silence, send them away by thinking about that one word. Let that word anchor you to the silent place so you can be reminded of whatever God might want to tell you.

CHAPTER 4:
THE TOO-MUCH-INFORMATION AGE

THINK

Our phones, computers, and the media are ever present in our lives. How has technology changed your daily life over the past twenty years? In what ways is your life better or less complicated because of things like texting, online news, social media, FaceTime, and apps? In what ways do those things complicate your life? How does the commandment about taking a Sabbath affect your digital life? Is that something you'd like to explore, or does it seem unnecessary or impossible to create a rhythm of rest from technology, media, and online information?

FEEL

I described my Airstream fantasy world in this chapter. Do you have a similar escape you turn to when real life becomes heavier than you would like it to be? Is there an activity that makes you feel the weight of life less? What emotions are you hoping to find on the other side of your escape from your real-life pressures? Have you sought to quench that thirst by meditating on the love of God instead?

ACT

Try taking a Sabbath from your phone and computer. Leave your phone at home when you go out one day or turn it off for a few hours of your day, but keep it in your bag in case of an emergency. Pay attention to what it feels like to be disconnected from the apps and texts and notifications that usually bombard you. Listen for God's presence and voice to shake the sugar tree of your daily life and sweeten the water He offers you with peace.

CHAPTER 5:
THE PERFECT STORM

THINK

In this chapter we read, "'For by one sacrifice he has made perfect forever those who are being made holy' (Hebrews 10:14 NIV). Given the lack of perfection we see in the people of Jesus, the word 'perfect' here can't mean being the most beautiful, talented, intelligent, admired, and esteemed person possible. It can't mean free from error, because the text says we are *being made holy*. Perfection is clearly different from holiness. The Greek word for 'perfect' in this passage is *teleioō*, and it means to be made complete or fulfilled. The Greek word here for 'holy' is *hagiazō*, which means to be purified, to be made free from sin, and to be internally renewed in your soul." What do you think is the difference between being made complete and being made pure? How would the world be different if all Christians pursued holiness while being secure in the completeness Christ has already accomplished?

FEEL

Imperfection is a natural and ubiquitous part of life, but it's rarely comfortable when our own flaws are exposed. Has there ever been a time when your own imperfections were on display? What was that experience like? Are there people in your life with whom you can be vulnerable? If there are, what is it about those relationships that allows you to do that? If not, what characteristics would you need in a friend to feel safe in that way?

ACT

First John 4:18–19 (esv) says that fear is evidence that we are not walking in God's love and wholeness: "There is no fear in love, but perfect love casts out fear. For fear has to do with punishment, and whoever fears has not been perfected in love. We love because he first loved us." Spend a few days (or more!) reading 1 John, Psalm 139, and John 15. Read them aloud, and when a particular phrase or verse strikes you as meaningful, write it down. Every day you do this, copy this quote in the journal below the passages you write and let it begin to form new faith in God to rescue you whenever you stumble in life: "What a comfort it is, this way of love! You may stumble on it, you may fail to correspond with grace given, but always love knows how to make the best of everything; whatever offends our Lord is burnt up in its fire, and nothing is left but a humble, absorbing peace deep down in the heart" (St. Therese of Lisieux, *Story of a Soul*).

CHAPTER 6:
PLEASE EXCUSE THE WOOD
PALLET WALL IN MY EYE

THINK

Have you ever been in a church that was consistently losing people or splitting apart in some way? What are some of the general reasons you think people leave churches? Why do you think people stay in a church even when others are leaving? What do you think is the connection between a single local church and the global Church? What do you think would help our churches be healthier, safer units of the greater global Church? How can you, as an individual, foster greater unity in the Body of Christ?

FEEL

Have you ever faced a real betrayal? Have you ever been the betrayer? What complications created that situation? What were the consequences? Was repentance offered, and was forgiveness attained? Can you see the love and grace of God weaving the pain of that wound into His own? Or have you had to box it up and wait for God's redemption of it at a later time? What have you learned about God and people through it all?

ACT

To create more hope in the world today, practice looking for people who are in need, and if you can provide for that need, do so. For example, while circling the parking lot at the grocery store, if spots are scarce and there is a car behind you also looking for a spot, pass up the good one so the person in the other car can have it. If you see a homeless person standing at a corner with a sign, roll down your window and say hello. Offer up a bottle of water or a prepackaged snack. If you notice a family struggling with unhappy children in a restaurant, smile at them, pay for their kids' food if you can, or just offer an empathetic word about how hard some days can be.

CHAPTER 7:
PRETTY THINGS AND THEIR
UGLY COUSINS AT HOME

THINK

How have consumerism and the accumulation of things shaped our current world? Why do you think minimalism and "tidying up" are so appealing to some people and not to others? What is the general effect of our spending and accumulating on our culture and society?

FEEL

What is the most beautiful thing you have ever seen? How did it make you feel? Did it cause you to connect with God in new ways? If it did, did that connection enhance the beauty of the thing? Did that connection help you understand God better? What did you feel as a result of this experience? How have you felt when you've returned to the beautiful thing again?

ACT

Take a moment today to set up a small communion table for yourself or your family. Read Luke 22 aloud and imagine the scene in your head. If you'd like, have some paper and colored pencils available and write or draw whatever the passage inspires you to create. Remember, whatever you create doesn't have to be worthy of a museum wall to bless God as a thing of beauty. Freely write or draw whatever the Holy Spirit inspires. Take a moment to confess any sins and ask for forgiveness or for any healing you may need from God. Commune with God in the space of your great need for Him. This is what Jesus came for, and it's His joy to be with you in this way. Then take the bread and remember the body of Jesus that carried the cross and was broken to make you whole. Take the wine or juice and remember His blood that was spilled out so you could be forgiven of all your sins. Say a quiet prayer of thanks to God and sit in the quiet for a few minutes to see if there is anything He would like to say to you.

CHAPTER 8:
GOD'S WILL IS LIKE A CHARCUTERIE BOARD

THINK

In considering the presence of evil in the world and why bad things happen to people, I've offered three possible conclusions in this chapter: (1) we moralize suffering and look to assign fault to the one who suffers; (2) we denigrate God's love for us either because He is not the good God we once believed Him to be or because we feel we are not worthy to receive good things from Him; or (3) we see every evil circumstance as a kind of "switchbacks of death" and look for the hidden holiness in our challenging circumstances. How do you think people who don't believe in God respond to the question of evil in the world? Are there other conclusions you have arrived at as you've tried to find a "why" for evil? What resources or thoughts have helped you when there seemed to be more wickedness than goodness in a particular circumstance?

FEEL

Has there ever been a time in your life when your proverbial plate seemed full of scary food? Did you eat it, or did you try to send it back to God and ask for something else? When you were facing the taste of bitter circumstances, what were you really hungry for from God? Deliverance? A miraculous resurrection of some kind? A blessing of hope? A happy ending? What has happened since then? Do you see how God's holiness was hidden in that plate, or do you still wonder why it had to be that way? What helps you endure the pain that still surrounds that experience?

ACT

If you are able, find a path or a hiking trail that is longer and steeper than you would typically choose. Commit to climbing it once a week for two months. As you climb, keep your mind present to the experience. Ask God to reveal Himself as you walk or run. Look for Him in your surroundings, listen for Him in your own body—the aches, the difficulty breathing, the longing to reach the end.

If you are unable to hike, commit to journaling at the end of each day for a month. Write down the most challenging moments and situations of your day. What weighs on you? What is life requiring you to carry that seems unjust or unfair? How can you offer those things to God? How can you enter into His love for you right there in that hard place and trust His ultimate plan is to bless you? After you journal, read Psalm 4 aloud and then sit in silence for five to twenty minutes while listening for God's comfort and presence.

CHAPTER 9:
HOUSTON, WE HAVE A PROBLEM

THINK

Given that Hebrews 11 is full of "failures," what is valuable about the kind of faith that expects God to fulfill His promises? If the end goal isn't necessarily the physical manifestation of the promise we are waiting for Him to fulfill, then what is? What is the purpose of faith in our prayer lives? How does our faith influence our spiritual development? Do you see evidence in the lives of people you know that a person of deep faith can have some kind of broader impact in the world?

FEEL

How have your own pride and insecurity played roles in your life? Do you tend toward thinking too highly of yourself or too lowly of yourself? How has that predisposition affected your relationships with God and other people? What practices, scriptures, or prayers help you become a Gospel-focused person when your ego is wounded or disturbed? Have you ever talked about your pride or insecurity with a safe friend or counselor? If you have, how did that person's perception of your struggle compare with your own inner experience?

ACT

Take out a piece of paper and divide it into three columns. Label the left column "Successes"; label the right "Failures"; and mark the middle column "To Be Determined." List out all the accolades and achievements you've attained in your life in the "Successes" column. Don't be shy—write anything that you remember as a positive reward for hard work or effort. Then in the "Failures" column, list out the dreams that didn't quite make it and all the times that the odds stacked against you ended up being too great to overcome. In the "TBD" column, write all the things you are attempting to achieve in your current circumstances. Proverbs 16:9 (NIV) says, "In their hearts humans plan their course, but the LORD establishes their steps." Take your lists to God in prayer, thanking Him for His help and blessings and offering Him your successes and failures while reflecting on the journeys that led to those end results. Close out your time of prayer by giving God your complete trust in His guidance over those things that have not yet become successes or failures and promise Him that you will give your all toward accomplishing these goals.

CHAPTER 10:
COMPARISON AND THE RICH UNCLE

THINK

In light of the NPR report about the study by psychology professor James Coan, why do you think people experienced greater peace before the electric shock when they had a friend with them? Do you think the opposite would be true—that people would have heightened anxiety if someone they perceived as an enemy were there in the room? What do you think the results of this study indicate about the importance of prioritizing friendship in our lives? Given that we have been designed and created by God, what do the results imply about His nature and our purpose?

FEEL

We read this in the chapter: "Connection and friendship help us endure the hard parts of life and give us peace during the pain." Has there ever been a particularly painful time in which a friend lessened the anxiety and struggle you faced? What specific actions on that person's part relieved the strain on you? Have you ever had to face a struggle alone? Were you able to feel the presence of God even though it seemed you shouldered the circumstance on your own?

ACT

One of the best ways to kill comparison in our lives is to express genuine admiration and honor toward others and their accomplishments. Make a list of your friends and family. Write three things you admire about each of them. Make a note alongside their names of any accomplishment or victory they have recently experienced. Pray a blessing over each of them, thanking God for the blessings He has already given them. Text or call them and tell them how much you admire and love them and that you are praying for them.

CHAPTER 11:
IN THE LIGHT OF AN ORDINARY DAY

THINK

Do you think it's true that everybody is famous somewhere? What is the difference between being famous in a local coffee shop or in your local community and being famous in a global sense? Would you ever want to be famous the way that actors and professional athletes and politicians are famous? Why or why not? What do you think is God's perspective on fame?

FEEL

The woman who anointed Jesus was apparently so open and connected to what her Lord was doing that she knew what He needed most. Her love for Him enabled her to move beyond the criticism of the people around her and extravagantly sacrifice a precious possession to join in what God was doing in the world at that time. Can you see what God is doing around you? Does your heart long to be a part of bringing redemption into the brokenness you witness in the world? If you aren't sure, pray and ask God for eyes that can see what He is doing and for the faith to give whatever you have that might be useful to Him.

ACT

We can't fully grasp our significance to God until we understand all it cost Him to redeem us. His love for you is great, but any unrepented sin is like a dam keeping His love from reaching you and filling you with the living water Jesus has promised us. Spend some time in prayer today asking God if there is any sin in your life you need to confess or repent of. Ask Him to show you any unforgiveness, resentment, fear, idolatry, hatred, selfishness, or jealousy that might be lurking in your soul. Refuse to avoid the holy place of asking God to forgive you, and enjoy the blessing of receiving the full measure of His love for you.

CHAPTER 12:
ALL WE DO IS WIN

THINK

In Revelation 12 we are told that the great accuser, who accuses us day and night before God, is eventually defeated by the blood of the Lamb and the word of our testimony. Can you see the power of story at work in your life currently? Have you seen evidence that the sacrifice Jesus made has affected the greater narrative of the world? How do you think the Gospel narrative has made the world a better place? How have people misused their testimonies and the Gospel to create additional pain and brokenness in an already broken world? How do you think all of this will compare with the day Jesus returns for us?

FEEL

When it comes to talking with or reaching out to strangers, whether you are socially forward or you prefer to retreat, do you ever consider if your motivation is less natural wiring and more a fear of failing God or failing people? Have you sought your Lord, who knew exactly when to engage and when to retreat, and asked Him to reveal His heart for the people you encounter? How willing are you to boldly engage someone if God asks you to do so? How prepared are you to hold your tongue if He directs you to be quiet and wait for His guidance and wisdom?

ACT

You have made it to the end of this book. I hope it feels like a dare to leap off a cliff into the clearest, bluest ocean you have ever seen. The last thing you can do, for the rest of today, all of tomorrow, and every day that comes after it is to engage your whole life in pursuing God and people with as much as you can offer them. You were made for this purpose, to love and be loved in a world that is starving for more of everything God has already provided for us all. Fill yourself every day with the living water of the God who has come to make you new, and then offer that water to everyone, everywhere. Be God's hands and feet, His heart and His light in the world.

NOTES

Chapter 3: Sit Down, Deborah

1. Dave Ward, "The Church, the Truth, and Women in Ministry," http://wesleyansermons.com/2019/09/23/the-church-the-truth-and-women-in-ministry-dr-dave-ward/

Chapter 4: The Too-Much-Information Age

1. Donna Frietas, *The Happiness Effect: How Social Media Is Driving a Generation to Appear Perfect at Any Cost* (New York: Oxford University Press, 2017), 230.

2. Nicholas Carr, *The Shallows: What the Internet Is Doing to Our Brains* (New York: W. W. Norton & Company, 2010) 131.3.

3. Adam Mabry, *The Art of Rest* (Surrey, England: The Good Book Company, 2018), 49.

Chapter 6: Please Excuse the Wood Pallet Wall in My Eye

1. Henri Nouwen, *The Wounded Healer* (New York: Image Books, 1979), 14–15.

Chapter 7: Pretty Things and Their Ugly Cousins at Home

1. Elaine Scarry, *On Beauty and Being Just* (Princeton, NJ: Princeton University Press, 2001), 11–12.

2. Scarry, *On Beauty*, 30.

Chapter 9: Houston, We Have a Problem

1. Mindy Kaling, *Is Everyone Hanging Out without Me?* (New York: Three Rivers Press, 2012), 7.

2. Zhang Jiuling, "Looking at the Moon and Thinking of One Far Away," accessed in "Three Classic Chinese Poems

about the Moon You Should Know," Chinese at Ease, http://chinese-at-ease.com/3-classic-chinese-poems-about-the-moon-you-should-know/.

3. Tim Keller, Blessed Forgetfulness, www.youtube.com/watch?v=0hgLeNwSXyo&list=PLc6sDrS4l3HcdFhwIjoPNfm2rPNvg7zUG&index=2.

4. Tim Keller, *The Freedom of Self-Forgetfulness* (La Grange, KY: 10Publishing, 2012), 33.

Chapter 10: Comparison and the Rich Uncle

1. Shane Blackshear, "Aaron Niequist, Author of *The Eternal Current*, Talks about a Practice-Based Faith," *Seminary Dropout*, podcast, 34:29, www.shaneblackshear.com/aaronniequist2/.

2. Barbara Bradley Hagerty, "Midlife Friendship Key to a Longer, Healthier Life," *Morning Edition*, March 16, 2016, hosted by Renee Montagne, NPR, transcript, www.npr.org/2016/03/16/470635733/midlife-friendship-key-to-a-longer-healthier-life.

Chapter 11: In the Light of an Ordinary Day

1. Ann Voskamp (@AnnVoskamp), Twitter, April 20, 2017, https://twitter.com/AnnVoskamp/status/855118929441804288.